into the light

by

JERRY SARGEANT

First published in Great Britain as an audiobook original in 2014

Copyright © Jerry Sargeant 2014

The moral right of this author has been asserted.

Typeset in Mercury and Trade Gothic LT Std

Editing and typesetting by UK Book Publishing

UK Book Publishing is a trading name of Consilience Media

www.ukbookpublishing.com

Published by Maximum Books

ISBN: 978-0-9929219-0-3

Contents

Thank you

"My mission in life is to motivate, touch the hearts of and inspire millions around the world to believe in themselves, stay strong in the face of adversity and build an armoury of faith deep in their soul that will protect them as they reach for the stars and unlock their true potential"– Jerry Sargeant

I dedicate this book to

YOU!

You are an amazing human being, you are beautiful, intelligent and kind. You are a being of light with infinite potential with a heart overflowing with love.

As you proceed on your inspirational journey to excel in the kingdom of the heaven you are creating, have faith at every turn, and the universe will be your trusted guide.

– Jerry Sargeant

When you are inspired by some great purpose, some extraordinary project, all your thoughts break their bonds; your mind transcends limitations, your consciousness expands in every direction and you find yourself in a new, great and wonderful world. Dormant forces, faculties and talents become alive, and you discover yourself to be a greater person by far than you ever dreamed yourself to be.

– Patanjali

Acknowledgements

I would like to thank my beautiful wife Laura and my two biggest teachers, my children. Aalayah and Joshua, you never cease to amaze me. I love you all with a passion, with all my heart, soul and every fibre of my entire being, always and forever.

I would like to thank the Universe, my guides and spiritual healers for working with me on this book. You have guided me and entrusted me with the task of passing this information onto humanity.

I want to take this opportunity to give special thanks and an abundance of love to Archangel Gabriel who first instructed me to lay my heart on the table, speak my truth and write these words. I would like to thank the angel Gabriel for allowing the flow of natural information to be channelled, in a way in which man must be superseded.

I thank all angels, fairies and beings of light that have guided and protected me throughout my life. With an abundance of love I give you thanks.

I would like to thank my friends who have supported me throughout my life journey. My love for you is eternal.

I would like to thank every human being in advance for being open, aware and listening to your divine guidance which will have, in turn, brought you into contact with this book.

I would like to thank Patricia Sterry from the Tree Of Life Centre for guiding me on my own personal journey and having the strength and patience to travel with me where many would have perished.

Introduction

I am writing this book after several messages from my spirit guides enabled me to see why this was necessary.

I was told that the messages in this book were of a more urgent nature and I must adhere to the protocols within my mission, the mission I chose as a light healer before embarking on this present journey in my earthly body.

As you read this book you will see some of the words will address you as if they were from me and other passages or sentences will be directly from source itself. When I refer to source I am acknowledging the depths of knowledge and the waves of wisdom that lie undisturbed in the invisible, the intelligence that created man, the Universe. Like other human beings I am a portal for consciousness to flow through. When one journeys Into the Light that portal opens and conscious awareness allows the Universal Intelligence to guide and direct those that listen.

I have been guided throughout the writing of this book just as you have been guided to find it and read it.

This book is about a journey Into the Light.
Your journey Into the Light.

Right now on Earth there is a revolution taking place. A spiritual revolution that is picking up pace as more and more human beings wake up and realise their true potential. For centuries the world we live in has been manipulated. The minds of men, women and children across the globe have been dumbed down. The low frequency information consumed by the human race for centuries has slowly, over time, produced a gigantic team of conforming robotic people and the essence of who and what we are has been covered in an illusionary reality that many human beings believe to be real.

Into the Light will uncover the answers to the universe and reveal the truth that you and every other human being wants to know.

Who am I and what is my true purpose?

So how did a man with a past like mine, who 10 years ago thought anyone who believed in God or anyone who claimed to be spiritual, was crazy or strange? How did my life turn from being in a dark and lonely world, to one where I changed the way in which I thought, stripped away the layers of darkness, dissolved my ego and stepped forth into the light?

How did I come from a life cloaked in darkness to a life where my mission in life is to motivate, touch the hearts of and inspire millions around the world to believe in themselves, stay strong in the face of adversity and build an armoury of faith deep in the soul, which will protect them as they reach for the stars and unlock their full potential.

In this book you will come to understand the relationship between the human body and the soul, the life force that lives inside. You will come on a journey with me and my spirit guides where, together, we will educate you on your earthly existence and the lessons you are learning along the way.

I am going to show you how amazing you truly are and how much potential power and natural ability you have within your own genetic make-up to advance in life in ways that you would never have thought possible.

You are about to go on a journey of self-discovery and as you read you will see the signs and the messages that are embedded within the following chapters. They will pose questions in your own mind which will make you think and give you keys. These keys are magical keys and they will unlock the good and greatness from within you. I have tears in my eyes right now as I am writing this. You are about to understand you.

I bet you're thinking but I understand me already. That's what I thought, but that's just your ego, speaking from fear of you finding out the truth about mankind, the human race and the infinite power which you possess. I am going to show you how to control your ego and believe in you as a free spirit, one of God's children, that is here on Earth right now to do your job. Your job and your work will become clear as you read these chapters.

By writing this book I am not asking for anything from you. I am simply giving you ideas, sharing my knowledge, beliefs and personal experiences with you. I am not wanting to be seen as a leader or some guru who claims to know something new. This information is not new; I have just gone through a process in my life which has made me aware of certain things. Important things that I want to share with you. Use the ideas and suggestions in this book as you will.

I, Jerry Sargeant, am acting as a messenger from the higher realms of the universal front. I am channelling messages that are being directed to each and every one of you special beings of light. You are about to realise why you came here and what you own personal mission is.

I am so, so excited for you. Your experience on Planet Earth and your connection to our mother is getting stronger and stronger, and the barriers between you and Mother Earth are being dissolved.

Reading this book will accelerate the process.

Let's do this.

Deep Knowledge

*Happiness is the meaning and purpose of life, the
whole aim and end of human existence.*

– Aristotle

Within us all there is a deeper understanding of the Universe we live
in. The animals, fish and birds all understand this knowledge and live
by its natural progression, each and every day. It enables them to live
in their environment and deal with daily life as best as they possibly
can.

Us human beings, well a large number of us anyway, do not have
the deeper understanding of our natural habitat and it forces
us to struggle with certain situations, especially where nature is
concerned. In situations that we may call unnatural, such as the
environment of a busy town or city and how we must act to stay safe,
even alive, is something we can adapt to quickly, but when nature
decides to act, without the deeper knowledge of the Universe, we will
perish in this bodily form.

If you live in a quiet town in New Zealand, where there is no traffic
and life is slow, you become accustomed to this. If a human being
who has lived within this environment all of his or her life, went to
the middle of London – or the capital of India, where life is even
more hectic and driving on the roads is a constant game of awareness
– the individual, used to his or her calm and slow habitat will have to
adapt very quickly or suffer the consequences.

When driving in India you need to be able to read the minds of many
men and women acting out their own part of this marvellous creation

we call life. Taxi drivers, market traders, women walking with their children, men and women shouting and haggling in the streets. All this is happening whilst you are trying to drive on a road you have never driven on before, with street names you may not understand, with a steering wheel on the other side of the car and yet you must be vigilant, and fully aware of all your surroundings, so as to not cause a fatal accident or be the fatality.

If you stay relaxed and become aware of your entire surroundings it's easy to adapt and stay safe. The minute you panic and become flustered, it all turns to custard. An animal that faces danger from nature will never remain in that situation until danger reaches its doorstep. An animal has a sixth sense, just like us humans do. Unfortunately, however, that sixth sense is lost in translation, somewhere between birth and growing up as a child. This happens through conditioning from external sources, such as our parents or school teachers. Animals, birds and fish, however, do not suffer from this issue. They are at one with their environment and have no external influences or an internal ego, to distract them from what they have known all their lives.

Take a tsunami, for example. It is an incredible event and if we as human beings were aware, just like animals, fish and birds are, we would get out of the way and watch it from a distance, in amazement as it travelled towards the shore. If we had the knowledge, the deeper understanding to sense its coming, we could revel in delight at the beauty of this amazing occurrence. Knowing humans and their behaviour, I am sure that above the water helicopters would be hovering, recording and streaming the event, live to TV stations across the globe. In fact, I am pretty sure that someone would have bought the rights to stream it over satellite television and charge you fifteen dollars to watch it live.

This is how out of touch human beings are with nature. We chop down millions of acres of forestry and what do we do with it? We turn it into newspaper, cover it in garbage and deliver mind-numbing information to the masses, furthermore distracting them from the essence of all life. We even have the gall to charge them for the newspapers, so in essence they are paying to destroy their own minds.

Furthermore the connections between human beings and nature are being destroyed. Putting up barriers all around so we start to believe that we as human beings are living in a strange land, a world where we do not belong. A world that we see as something that is not us. We grow up with hostility towards the world and when a tsunami hits and other humans die, and a town or beach resort is destroyed, we call it a tragedy and a disaster. If only we held onto the deep knowledge that's within us all, we would view nature as a part of our soul, and we would see ourselves as an extension of the Universe, living in harmony, and playing out the magnificent game of life.

If we were aware of the deep seated knowledge that lies within us, we would get out of harm's way and watch on with awe. The knowledge and wisdom carried forward for millions of years, is at the core of each and every soul that graces this planet. As you travel into the light with me or maybe further in for some of you, the stains of the outside world will be washed away forever and the deep seated knowledge, held back by the attachment to the material world, will re-appear and your life will become whole once more.

In the words of the Buddha, Trishna is the root cause of Dukkha. In other words, suffering (Dukkha) comes from attachment (Trishna). Attachment to the illusionary world is the cause of unhappiness, a lack of love and peace and the daily stresses that we manufacture in our minds, to give ourselves a sense of belonging and identity in this crazy world we live in. Once you journey towards the light and enter with your heart and soul, the mysteries that once cloaked your view of reality will be lifted like the veil of the beautiful woman stood before you at the altar, the woman you are about to spend the rest of your life with.

Life will become clear and your vision will be free. Your dreams will be whole and your heart will be full. Into the light we go.

In A Nutshell

Things do not change; we change.

– Henry David Thoreau, *writer and philosopher*

It's important that I give you a brief overview of my life so that you get an understanding of where I came from, the point at which I am in my life now and more importantly, the journey and the transitional period where I changed my entire outlook on life.

I was born on March 8th 1978. My birth mother had told her parents that she would be going to college in Cheltenham, England. The real reason she was going to Cheltenham was to give birth to me. My birth father did not know about me and still does not. As the result of a one night stand, my birth mother could not face telling her parents about the pregnancy, so cooked up a story and told her parents she was going to college.

I was born at approximately 4pm in the afternoon. It was a horrific pregnancy for my mother; she was treated badly both physically and mentally. As soon as I was born I was whisked away and there was no bonding process. I was fostered straight away and after a few foster homes I was eventually adopted.

I grew up in Gloucester, a few miles away from Cheltenham Town, where I was born. My adoptive parents worked very hard to put a roof over my head and food on the table. I had a sister who was also adopted from another family. We were your average two point four, middle class family. My parents loved me as much as they could. My mother especially struggled with me. I think they thought they would get a readymade baby in a box, with full instructions, which conformed when they spoke. I was totally the opposite. I rebelled wherever I could.

I was a very angry child and the only thing that kept me out of trouble was rugby – I loved it with a passion. At the age of fourteen I was banned for one year. I was sent off for fighting on the pitch and then continued to fight on the touchline, after one of their players made a remark. I had to appear in rugby court and was banned for one year. I didn't know how to handle this as rugby was my life.

I turned to drink and drugs and associated with a different group of lads. After numerous trips to the police station to pick me up, after all sorts of different incidents, the relationship with my mother got out of hand. I moved out of home and lived in a rough part of town with my friend. The rave scene (parties in fields, fuelled by Ecstasy and Acid) was rife and I was travelling all over England partying and having a blast, without a care in the world.

One day I was at home, in our flat, and I was doing the washing up. The music was loud and I did not hear the door open. I felt something in my back. I turned around and saw an older man with gold teeth and dreadlocks pointing a knife into my stomach. He took me off in his car, with some other guys. They took me to the petrol station, filled up a can and told me they were going to burn me alive. We drove around for a few hours and eventually we stopped. I saw my chance and ran.

When I got home the flat was empty. They had stolen everything. It was just a ploy to get me out of the house so their friends could go in and rob us. Anyway, being driven around for a few hours thinking I was going to be burned alive was a good wake-up call. I knew I had to change my situation. I believe that everything that causes pain in this world is perfect. One has to feel pain in order to know what one does not want and so move in the opposite direction.

I got a job, through an agency, working at a local ice cream factory. My plan was this: save up as much money as I could in one year, buy an old camper van and then go off travelling around Europe with my girlfriend at the time. Both of us saved for the year. I worked twelve hour nights, six days a week and saved a few thousand pounds, by the end of the year. We bought the van and were set to leave. What took place next was a miracle; actually it was the Universe, in all its glory, redirecting me, back on track. I will explain this in detail later on as you journey deeper Into the Light.

The event that took place led me to the Canary Islands in Tenerife, where I became a timeshare salesman, working for a high profile criminal organisation. I became very good at my job, mastered the art of sales and earned lots of money.

Tenerife is renowned for being home to any British man or woman who is either on the run from the authorities themselves or simply up to no good. It was a very easy step for me to get involved with lots of other criminal activities. As well as selling timeshare, I got involved in drug smuggling, gun trafficking, unlicensed boxing and a few other unmentionable dealings with interesting characters.

None of these I am proud of but at the same time none of them I would ever change, as each event, circumstance or situation helped shape and mould me into the human being I am today. I learned so many valuable lessons and took away an abundance of knowledge and wisdom, related to life itself.

By the time I was nineteen years old I had saved more than half a million pounds, by the time I was twenty one I was broke. I had the equivalent of two thousand pounds to my name. My company had been shut down by Spanish police and the owners sent to prison for thirty million pounds' worth of timeshare fraud.

By this time I had met my future wife and we had had our first child. My wife is from Romania and getting married was difficult for many reasons. I had to sneak my wife and daughter back into the UK, so we could get married. This is a whole other story – however it's not mine to tell.

Once back in England I started a property investment company. We designed a new product and took it to the market place. Within the first year we had taken eleven million pounds in service fees and life was really good. The problem was my ego was in full control and I was very materialistic. We had an office in Mayfair, an office in Marbella, sixty staff and flew across the globe, attending property exhibitions, meeting clients and making money. I was always striving for success, searching for happiness but always looking in the wrong place. I was always searching externally.

In 2004, the property market took a downturn and we hadn't prepared for this. We lost everything, and more importantly so did most of our clients. I went from driving a range of fast cars, wearing expensive watches and tailor-made suits and dining in the finest restaurants, to borrowing fifty pounds from my friend to feed my family one day. This was a real test of character.

Really it was a blessing in disguise, because I was becoming far too egotistical and driven by money and material objectives and for this my family suffered.

After this, I went back to the streets, trying to survive for a while, and then I thought enough was enough after a serious altercation that could have cost me my life. I know in my heart that my angels looked after me that day and I am eternally grateful.

I went and spoke with companies in London that sold a range of different products. I offered them my services in exchange for a percentage of the profits if all went well. It did and I crawled back up to a place where I could breathe and eventually got back on top.

A few years passed and my wife and I decided we wanted to move out of England and had made New Zealand our first choice. To get into the country we needed a business work visa which would have taken some time. I had become passionate about the environment, so decided to set up a company called Green World New Zealand. We would use the money I had made recently to build low carbon emission homes, on Maori land. We would make them affordable, healthy and environmentally friendly.

We worked on the project for three years prior to arriving in NZ. All the plans were drawn up, the land was in place and I flew my UK partners out to NZ for a big presentation. It all went well and the local council agreed to give us planning permission. What happened next was a real curveball. I made the local chairman of the Marae (the place we were to build the houses upon) a director of my company. This was the wrong thing to do. It would have meant him earning money and so his family would not give their blessing on the land and allow it to be built upon. That was it. Goodnight Green World New Zealand.

It was not the best position to be in. A new country, a business that had fallen apart and most of our money had been spent on the project. We were relying on the build of the project to release new finances. It actually turns out that this was divine intervention and that I was not supposed to build the project. I had a greater task at hand but this would not be realised until much later on.

From here on in I went and started a personal training business to bring some cash in. I hired some space at a local gym and it went very well. After several months the gym owner saw that I was doing very well and wanted more money off me, and so put my rates up. I said no. Her response was, you are no longer welcome at the gym.

As I had nowhere to train my clients and did not want to adhere to the rules set out by other gyms I decided to open my own. So Fierce Fitness was born. What I didn't realise at the time was that the Universe was priming and preparing me for my real purpose here on this planet. At the gym we helped people and I really enjoyed seeing the changes in people's lives. I also appeared on television a number of times, doing exercise routines for the viewers at home. This helped me build my confidence.

After two years, we were getting itchy feet, both my wife and I. We knew we had to do something greater than this but didn't know what. We dealt some fairy cards, which give you an outlook on past, present and future. They said we would be travelling soon and also going on holiday. In May, we had been denied a new working visa under our gym. We appealed, climbed the hurdle laid down in front of us and were denied a second time. We thought let's go on holiday and see if we can get some answers. It was very strange after all. Being denied for reasons that were easily reconciled and justified.

We booked a holiday to Moorea, a small island near Tahiti. We were at Auckland airport and about to board our plane and a message came out over the tannoy: your plane is delayed one hour. The first thought that came into my head was, read your book. It was a book I had read maybe a thousand times before. I had been prompted several times over the last few weeks to read it but totally ignored the Universe. Well now a whole plane full of beautiful human beings ready to go on holiday had been delayed, just so I could read this book. I think I'd better listen, I remember thinking to myself.

I picked up the book and read a few pages and the most intense visualisation occurred. I saw my whole life flash in front of my eyes. Everything that had ever happened in my life, within five to ten seconds, flashed before my eyes like a video reel playing the movie of my life. I looked up at my wife and said I know what I have to do. I have to write a book to inspire other people.

And so that was it; I started writing and from there speaking publicly about my life, the events within it and more importantly what I had learned. That is what you are about to find out. This is a short synopsis of my life, outlining some important events that helped shape and mould me and give you an idea of how my life has unfolded.

You will notice that there was a turning point when my focus changed. After losing my property business I went down the route of low carbon emission homes. My attention shifted from a dark world to one with an intention of light and doing good for others, and not just thinking about me and my ego.

There was an event that took place, which was the focal point, clear and concise, brought about by the power that knows more than you or I, the power that is you and me. It was at this crucial moment my life started to change.

The Angry Old Man

*When we learn to say a deep, passionate yes to the things
that really matter, then peace begins to settle onto our
lives like golden sunlight sifting to a forest floor.*

– **Thomas Kinkaide,** *artist*

So how did I change my ways and come from the depths of darkness
and despair to live a life in which I am happy, motivate others to
succeed and have found love and personal happiness?

In 2004 I had just lost my business. It was my second attempt at
creating a prosperous life for me and my family and it all turned
to custard after the property market took a downturn at the end
of 2004. My business went into administration, I lost every asset I
possessed and every drop of cash I had was stripped away until the
onion was just the centrepiece. Luckily I had my family and they still
loved me.

I went from having millions to having nothing within a matter of
weeks. The times were challenging.

After this happened I was back to my old tricks of selling drugs on
the street to keep a roof over my family's head. I did what I thought
was right at the time to stay alive. A few months after my business
had collapsed I had a run in with a local gang that could have been
the end of my life but my angels and guides came to my rescue. At
the time I just thought I was lucky. This was a sign from the Universe
to stop doing what I was doing and I needed to find an alternative
road.

One day soon after, I was sitting watching television on a Sunday evening and something happened that was to change the course of my life. It was an encounter with the paranormal, not me personally but my wife. What it did however was wake me up and show me that there is something else out there and it led me on a journey of self-discovery that would change the course of my life forever.

It was a Sunday evening and Laura, my wife, had put the kids to bed and taken an early night herself. I was downstairs watching television. Laura came downstairs, with a look of worry on her face and I said, 'What's up?' She looked at me and said, 'Every time I close my eyes I hear voices and see dark images. It's like someone is trying to take me away.'

I asked what she wanted to do about it. In my mind I was thinking what are you on about? Has my wife gone crazy? She said she wanted to call her friend who was a local priest. So she did and the lady was around our house very quickly. She dowsed the house and put crosses up and I just sat in the chair thinking to myself, this is like something out of a film.

Anyway, my wife became calmer after talking to her friend and went to bed. The next day I told a friend of mine about this incident. Straight away he said you should call this lady and he gave me a name and telephone number of a lady called Trish and told me to call her.

I called her immediately but she didn't answer. She called back shortly after and I told her the story. She asked me where we lived and so I told her, '316 Richmond Road'. She asked if I had been knocking any walls down and I said, 'No, we rent the house but an extension has been built on the back.' She told me to wait a moment and the phone went quiet. Then she said to me, 'You have an angry old man in your house.'

An angry old man I thought to myself. What is going on here?

I said to her, 'OK what are we going to do about it?'

'I will get rid of him' was the reply.

We spoke for a few more moments and then I hung up.

I was thinking an angry old man, whatever. This is crazy. An angry old man.

So I went home and saw Laura and explained that I had spoken to this lady and told her what had happened and that she reckoned that there was an angry old man in the house. Laura turned to me and said, 'I know, I've seen him.'

I couldn't believe it. Two people, who have never met each other, have no common friends, live one hundred and twenty miles apart from each other, and could never ever have spoken, are both telling me exactly the same thing. There must be something to this, I thought. That was it. I phoned Trish back up and made an appointment. Trish owns, and still does to this day, The Tree of life Centre in Gloucestershire. They do past life regression therapy.

I went there two or three times a week for years. This was the start of a new beginning in my life. A new chapter. It was this incident that led me on the most important journey of my life, one where I looked in the most important place on earth for all the answers. I started to look inside of myself. I went on the most incredible journey of my life and started to understand myself for the first time ever.

We all get messages and signs from the Universe and I had received lots up until this point, over the years, but I was unaware, didn't pay attention or was driven by a material loving world that consumed my mind and not once did I listen. It took an angry old man from another dimension who had entered our house along ley lines – energy lines that spirits, particularly stuck in the in-between world, travel down. Our rented house happened to be built on one, and I am so glad it was.

Maybe that's why we moved there in the first place. Maybe that's why my business went bust so I was forced to move because the Universe had this house lined up for me, knowing that this event would happen and I would go on this amazing journey and find out for the first time in my life who Jerry Sargeant really was.

Maybe? There is no maybe about it. The Universe knew exactly what was happening. This was orchestrated down to the letter. It was calculated and executed with precision. I had to go through the darkness in my life for a number of reasons, the main one being to enable me to tell my story and help others move from the darkness into the light, just like I did. I was sent on my mission, a mission I had agreed to before entering my human body in this time and space.

Once I had seen and experienced enough, the Universe decided to put me and my family in this house and let this experience happen. I was too egotistical and unconnected to enable this angry old man to affect me so my wife came to my aid and sacrificed herself for me. I love you, Laura, with all my heart.

Wake Me Up

There are two great days in a person's life
– the day we are born and the day we discover why.

William Barclay, *twentieth-century Scottish theologian*

This was the start of a new chapter in my life. I had been stuck in the depths of darkness up until this point, going around in circles, always looking for the next challenge, or something to fulfil my needs as a man. I was always looking outside of myself for the answers and I was soon to realise that there is only one place to look, and that is inside.

Here on earth right now we are at a critical stage of evolution and the level of group consciousness needs to elevate. There is a lack of light here on this planet and if human beings carry on as they are, being consumed by their own thoughts and driven by the ego, I am not sure whether we can sustain ourselves, and the human race may become extinct.

The good news is that over recent years there has been a major shift in awareness and many other individuals, myself included, have woken up, become aware of the truth and started to spread the word and raise global consciousness.

For many years, the egoic mind has ruled the minds of men and women, far and wide, and has created patterns and thought forms that have become ingrained in our souls, not just from this present lifetime, but from many others before it, spanning thousands of years. As human beings today we are conditioned. The good news is that we can break these forms of conditioning, harness our ego and release a power. A power that lies within us all. A power that is so strong and pure, that it will guide us and ensure our safety if we allow it to.

First we have to become aware of this power. Once we become aware then we are able to connect with it. At this point we can start a new way of life, one that human beings on this planet experienced thousands of years ago, in what was known as the Golden Age. We are entering a time and a space where we are at a critical stage of evolutionary growth and we have two choices. We can, firstly, raise our global vibration and return once again to the Golden Age. The other option is to fall deeper into the dark hole we are trying to climb out of and if we do, who knows what the result will be. It doesn't bear thinking about.

I firmly believe that the awareness on this planet is rising and we will pull through. It has to. What gives me reassurance is the fact that a man like me can change his ways, wake up and see life for what it really is. I took a one hundred and eighty degree u-turn in my life, to come from one of darkness and destruction to one of love and light. If I can do it, anyone can.

When the angry old man came into our house it ignited something within me, a spark that led me on a journey of self-discovery. We all need motivation or a little inspiration to kick start us in the right direction. The angry old man was mine. I am so grateful, but after all it was perfection. A mind that knew more than I did, more than you or any other human being on this planet does, guided me, and the angry old man from another dimension was the tool in which this invisible but powerful force chose to use and operate on me with. Total perfection.

I am going to share with you through this book some of my life experiences that have led me to think in the way I think these days. You will see what happened to me and why I woke up. It was not something that happened overnight. To get to where I am took effort and practice and plenty of willpower. There were times when my ego kicked back in and tried to destroy the good I had done, by trying to take back control of my mind. It takes constant effort at the start of the journey to let the light shine through and blast away the years of conditioning. Eventually though, with enough effort on my part and soon to be yours, you too will re-connect with the inner you. The conscious you. The light within you that is so powerful. The energy source that made you and manifested through you into human form.

Some call it God; I call it many names. The Universe, source, light source, formless substance, presence or awareness. It all means the same. What this force is, is a feeling. It has no start, middle or end. It is infinite and will never die.

Sitting on Your Cloud

The winds of grace are always blowing, but you have to raise that sail.

- Sri Ramakrishna, *nineteenth-century Indian saint*

We are eternal spiritual beings of light. We have many incarnations in a bodily form and have had many other lives in other spiritual dimensions where the energy is totally different. It takes great courage to embark on a journey here on Planet Earth as our souls, our spirit, when we are at source, can see what it's like down here and know the challenges we will face with such dense and unharmonious energy.

We make sacrifices, however. We all do in different shapes and forms, dependent on the life that we are choosing to lead. I chose a lifetime where I would experience difficult situations and extreme mental and physical pain at the start of my journey to enable me to fulfil the second part of my life, on Mother Earth, this time around.

I am a light worker here to help and motivate others on their own personal journeys. I am here to help raise awareness and the level of consciousness here on Planet Earth. Over recent years Earth's energy has become so dark and dense that most human beings are living a life which is nowhere near a life that a light soul of energy should be living. It's the reason so many of us here on Planet Earth struggle so much, and go within ourselves, more importantly, our minds. We go to a place where we lose our spiritual connection and life becomes dull and slow and we feel very heavy.

We chose this when we were sitting on our cloud, up in heaven, waiting to come down and play this real life game of chess. Some people call it heaven; I call it the spirit world or ball of light. A dimension or another realm that is saturated in purity and peace. It's such a beautiful place and if only we human beings all understood what it was like there we would have no fear of death.

Souls that chose to come down into this life we are living right now have sacrificed themselves to help save Mother Earth. Mother Earth has feelings, she is made up of energy just like you and me. She has feelings and so do all of the other elements that make up our world: the trees, plants, animals, fish, flowers and every other object such as the rocks. They all feel and vibrate at a frequency and can feel the pain that Mother Earth is going through when pollution spills into her rivers and streams.

We need to start waking up and realising that we are not just here in this earthly body to go through the motions of life. Life is much more than you know. So much of humanity works to survive on this planet that has so much else to offer. Why would you want to sit on the treadmill of life when you have so much to offer others and have so much to enjoy yourself?

You are hearing and reading this message as you needed to hear this message. Your internal guidance system will have directed you to this book to enable you to break free. I am being directed to write it just as you are being placed in the perfect situation to find it and read it.

You chose this life and if you were not aware up until this point that you had specific tasks to accomplish in this lifetime, now you know. It's time to start looking inside yourself and asking questions about what great possibilities there are here on Earth for you do. Inside your mind, heart and soul you have a collection of historic records that contain all the answers to the mystery of life. The more you start to communicate with your higher self, the more knowledge you will be able to download, from the files contained in your subconscious mind.

Find a quiet space and re-open the lines of communication, by asking yourself whatever questions you feel are right. Start exploring and you will go on an adventure more exciting than any holiday you could ever imagine. The information you are about to unlock is priceless, more rewarding than anything you have ever known.

I am so happy for you. Love every moment and enjoy this magical journey.

750 Past Lives

Whether you are aware of them or not, whether you recognise them as spiritual or not, you probably have had the experience of silence, or transcendence, or the Divine – a few seconds, a few minutes that seem out of time; a moment when the ordinary looks beautiful, glowing; a deep sense of being at peace, feeling happy for no reason. When these experiences come... believe in them. They reflect your true nature.

– Sri Sri Ravi Shankar, *spiritual teacher and humanitarian*

So we sit on our cloud and choose the life we will enter into. How do we know what that life will bring? That life is in the future so how do we know what's going to happen? How can we choose something that has not taken place yet?

Past, present and future are all one. Where you are stood right now, all around you there are lots of other worlds and lives being lived in these worlds. There are many other dimensions that are not available to your naked eye as your energy is too dense to see them.

Past, present and future has already happened. Take déjà-vu for example. How many times have you been going about your day and you do something and say, oh my gosh, I've been here before? I dreamt about this? Or, however you saw the situation prior to it happening, this has been an event you have experienced already in your mind. How is that possible? The reason it's possible is because it has already happened. Quite often your subconscious mind takes you forward in life to certain circumstances or events to prepare you for what is happening. Ninety nine percent of the time, most of us can't remember, but every now and again we get déjà-vu.

The Universe is one gigantic amalgamated chasm of intricacy. A maze of lives and dimensions all happening at the same time in unison with the reality of our channelled network of light. As I mentioned we are all here for a purpose and that purpose in life is to raise the level of consciousness here on Mother Earth.

We all play different roles with a myriad of outcomes. The outcomes can change through the choices we make. If a human being gets sucked up into the darkness on this realm then quite possibly they will live a life and learn lessons that that particular life throws at them. Regardless of what choices they make it will be perfect. The Universe just flows naturally with the choices each and every one of us make. There does come a point, however, when the Universe and its light workers have to step in and take action.

Right now, here on Planet Earth, we are moving into a better space, slowly but surely and we are picking up speed all the time due to the caring nature and courage of those that have been chosen for the role. Behind the scenes there is a revolution taking place. A revolution more important than any your history has ever shown you. Your vibration is rising as you read these words and you will find that you start to naturally take a greater interest in the planet and its wellbeing. You may start to find yourself picking up rubbish that someone else has left behind and feel exhilarated about that fact, as you are helping Mother Earth gain in health. You are ridding her from the toxins humans leave behind.

Just as you can go forward in time so can you go back. Each of us that is alive on Earth at this present moment in time has had approximately seven hundred and fifty past lives. I have been into many of mine and experienced the traumas and happiness of each one. Just as we human beings in this lifetime are patterned from a young age so are our souls over time, through lifetime after lifetime. We can carry energies and experiences within our make-up, from one lifetime to another and it can affect us in a positive or negative way.

My parents used to say to me when they saw someone with money, 'flash git or 'stuck up bugger'. Hearing these kind of remarks growing up you start to think that all people with money must be horrible people and the pattern of 'money is bad' starts to be etched into your subconscious mind.

The same happens in past lives. If you have an experience where you lose a family member for example and don't deal with it constructively it can carry forth into this lifetime and you may be faced with the challenge again, until you do deal with it constructively.

That's another reason we come back to Mother Earth and live in a dense bodily form. It's for our own soul-growth. We learn so many lessons whilst we are here, in this time and space and each time we do, we grow spiritually. If we don't learn our lessons then we often come back again, choosing a similar life, because we know we have to learn that lesson. When we incarnate, we lose memory of being on our cloud, choosing the life we did, and just grow up learning all over again.

There is so much more to life, you see, and now you know this very fact you too can start making choices. You can make them with awareness of the greater purpose of each and every soul on this planet. We need to make the choices that help us grow. We should never feel pressured to make a decision – if it doesn't feel right then don't do it.

We all have an internal navigational system: our gut instinct. It's always right, it never lets us down. You just have to be prepared to listen and take action when necessary. You have a number of different outcomes to this life you are living; some are good, and some are not so good. Some of them, however, are breathtaking, in a positive sense. Why not start searching your soul for the answers right now? Just do it and create the life for yourself that you so rightly deserve, as a being of light that originated from the divine source, heaven.

What Is Past Life Regression Therapy?

God is the friend of silence. See how nature – trees, flowers, grass – grows in silence; see the stars, the moon and the sun, how they move in silence... We need silence to be able to touch souls.

– Mother Teresa

So we all have had a significant number of past lives that have helped shape and mould us into the spiritual beings that we are today. So how do you access your past lives and how does going back to that distant place benefit you?

Well actually it's not that distant. It may be one thousand years ago that I was an Aztec Indian but I can access that past life within seconds. I can enter my computer files that are stored inside my subconscious mind and have a look. Just as you open a document from your hard drive, on your computer, so can you access the files in your mind.

You just have to relax and be prepared to travel the road. Sometimes it's rocky and sometimes it's smooth. Either way you have to be open minded and let your thoughts flow, in time with your breath, and the beat of the universal substance.

When I went into my first past life I did so with my eyes closed and with much help and guidance. Now I can do it whilst I am driving and see with my mind's eye, as clear as day, what is happening. It's just like a cinema screen playing in your mind. If I asked you to sit where you are right now, take a few slow deep breaths and imagine yourself lying on the beach of your dreams, relaxing, you would have a clear picture in your mind. You probably did just then as you were reading this. If I said that the waves were rolling in off the crystal blue ocean and the sun was beating down with a cool breeze brushing against your face, you would probably see and feel that immediately.

Just as you see yourself lying on the beach, so will you see the aspect of your soul in the lifetime you enter. So how exactly do you enter these lives?

When I was learning I had my real life angel, Patricia Sterry, guiding me every step of the way. I was very lucky to have such an awesome teacher. I would sit in my chair opposite Trish and then she would ask me to take a few deep breaths, and then imagine a golden bubble all around me. I would then see a colour coming into that bubble (which would represent something, a mood for example). I would breathe that colour into my body until it had engulfed every part of my body from my fingers to my toes.

After this, I would see a box on the floor next to me. I would put any worries, fear, troubles or any negative emotion into that box. I would then put the lid on and watch it float away and turn into light and positivity and allow it to be used for good wherever necessary.

After this I would see a flame. He was called my heart flame. This is my higher self and who I spoke with throughout my journey. He always answered honestly and directly.

Next I would see a heart with a smile and a pathway leading up to it. I would climb through the smile and in through the heart. On the other side I would now be standing in a field. Now I was inside my subconscious mind and could communicate with it perfectly, access any files etc. Next Trish would ask me to look for a tree in the field. Different trees resembled different things. For example, an oak tree would resemble strength.

Once I had found the tree I would walk up to it and step inside. My feet would sink down into the roots and become part of Mother Earth and my arms and hands would go into the branches and become a part of Father Sky. I would then ask my subconscious mind, or heart flame, to take me to whichever level he felt necessary.

Once there I would walk down a pathway, up to a door and through it. Once on the other side I would be in a place. It could be a street, a building, a jungle, an Indian teepee, a mine in Africa, a war zone, a family party. The list is endless. I have been into so many past lifetimes it's incredible and each one has helped me grow spiritually, in this lifetime and as a soul on my own special journey.

The main purpose of my regressions was to deal with all the dark aspects of my soul and strip them away until I was left with the purity in the middle, the goodness that I wanted to share with the rest of the world. It took me a long time to get to that point because I had so much darkness to clear. There were times when I broke down crying and thought how could I carry on? Why don't I just go back to my life of crime and darkness and take the easy road. It's only easy on this planet because the energy is so dark and dense but each and every one of us can rise above it. We all have the strength and the power to do it.

You have to believe in yourself, take action and start the process. Your journey has already started. The reason I know this to be true, is the simple fact that you are reading this book. You would not want to step forward into the light, with me, if you weren't reading this book. You are, however, reading it so it must be true. It's universal perfection. You are on the right path; whatever has happened in your life up until this point does not change the fact that you have made certain choices and have been led to purchase and read the words, within the cover of Into the Light.

You are understanding more and more and your life is changing already. You are absorbing the messages from the Universe, into your mind and are arming yourself with the very tools needed to make your life better and better, and to fulfil your universal mission.

The German Soldier

There are only two ways to live life. One is as though nothing is a miracle. The other is as though everything is a miracle.

– Albert Einstein

When I first walked into The Tree Of life Centre in Gloucestershire and met Trish I didn't know what to expect. Travelling the road I had up until this point in my life had made me sceptical about things like this. To be honest, I pretty much pooh-poohed any idea of God or spiritual activity and thought ghosts were utter nonsense. If it wasn't for the angry old man I would never have made it to the barn that day, and into Trish's room.

When I was growing up and when I lived in Tenerife in my late teens in the Canary Islands and a huge part of my life was drinking and taking drugs. I was always out partying and getting up to mischief.

Each and every time I would go out I would get drunk and start putting on these German accents and torment everyone in sight. I am not, when sober, able to put on a German accent the way I can when I have had a skinful of liquor. I had videos of myself, that mates had filmed and I actually looked and sounded very German. In fact my whole demeanour changed – I really did look German.

They say that when you are under the influence of alcohol and or certain narcotics you are able to connect with your higher self on a deeper level. It unlocks some kind of barrier that is put up by our conscious minds and stops us from being and seeing who we really are. The files that store all our valuable information from decades and centuries ago is unlocked because our minds relax and channels are opened and the information runs freely.

Some of the greatest creators of all time have produced their very
best work when they have been under the influence of alcohol.
The very same men in the end, however, have killed their minds by
overuse and indulgence. Vincent van Gogh, Ernest Hemingway and
many other well-known writers and artists have exacerbated their
most prominent artefacts through the use of alcohol.

I am not saying that you need to drink to become creative and
produce masterpieces and find your true path. The point I am trying
to make is that when you are under the influence you unlock the real
you.

When I first walked into the barn and sat down with Trish she said
all she could see was a German soldier. I was Jerry Sargeant but what
was prominent to Trish was my direct correlation to the abstract
image of my personality. She saw me in full uniform, as I was when
I was a German Soldier in the Second World War. That was my last
incarnation before the one I am living today. I explained to Trish that
when I used to drink I would pretend to be German. I didn't know
why, but it just felt very natural.

'Yes, it makes sense,' she replied. 'I can see you clearly as a German
soldier. Would you like to go and see what happened in that lifetime?'

'Yes,' I replied.

So we went about what became the ritual, before each and every
regression. Once in the tree I went down to the level that connected
me with my German life in 1943. I was in the middle of a war zone
and there were buildings being blown up everywhere. I was trying to
get to a building, a few hundred yards away, to rescue a family that
had been trapped inside.

I was about twenty seven years old, clean shaven, unlike today, and determined to reach this family and help them out. When I reached the building and went inside I realised they were English, but still I wanted to help them. Another one of my German friends or so-called friends was there. He was a fellow soldier and was unhappy to see my kind and gentle nature towards the foreign slaves. He pulled out his gun and was about to shoot them, but before he did so I shot him straight in the head.

This wasn't the only lifetime that I had taken a life. It was, however, the last. I have been in so many situations in this lifetime where it could have easily happened again but for some reason I always found myself absconding from the situation with my conscience clear. A huge challenge for me in this lifetime has been to come from the dark to the light. I was trying as a German soldier, by rescuing the family in the building, but I still took a life.

I had to come back into this life I am living right now to be tested again. I am so, so happy and so grateful that I became aware in this lifetime, and listened to my guides and my angels and every other helping hand along the way that has helped steer me and guide me to a heavenly place, where violence is a distant memory.

I no longer drink and haven't taken drugs for many years. I owe this to my wife and children and my spirit guides who play me like a piano now that I am aware. Life is truly fantastic. The cosmic zone that we are travelling through is a foregone conclusion, for all that are willing to take on board the message of the divine light warriors.

Spiritual Warrior

There is a vitality, a life-force, an energy, a quickening that is translated through into action...Keep the channel open.

– Martha Graham, *twentieth-century dancer and choreographer*

It wasn't long after meeting Trish that she told me I would become a spiritual warrior. I asked what that meant, and she told me that in many of my previous lifetimes I have been a warrior and have carried that warrior image into this lifetime. This time around, however, she said I would be fighting very hard for a good cause and on a side for which I have not usually been accustomed to fighting.

This side was the light. I would be a spiritual warrior crusading for the universal growth and the growth of humanity itself.

At this time I was still in a place in my life that was so far away from what I was being told. At that time I couldn't really comprehend it, but something inside of me actually resonated with what she was saying. My tough exterior was putting up a fight, my ego wasn't having any of it but something deep inside me knew this to be true.

It was around 2006 and I was making money, good money and one day I had the inspiration to donate some money to charity. At my next appointment with Trish I told her that I wanted to donate a percentage of the money I was earning to charity and if she knew of any that would be good for me give to. She knew a lady who was working in Africa, building schools, hospitals and infrastructure in general and that she would be happy for the funds and also Trish knew that the funds would get used in the correct way. The people would actually benefit from our donation.

I became like Robin Hood in my eyes and I absolutely loved it. I donated a percentage of the money I was receiving, through Trish and remained anonymous. It was so good when the letters came through saying what they had done with the money. It was amazing to hear how many people that we had helped, and the feeling of joy and happiness that filled my heart and my soul was a real game-changer.

It was during the next twelve months that I really started to work hard in my past life regression therapies and strip as many dark elements away from my soul as possible, so that I could become the light warrior that I came to Earth to become, the spiritual warrior that both Trish and my heart flame told me I would be.

Having the opportunity to donate that money, enabled me to feel what it was like to give and instil faith into the hearts and souls of local communities that needed help, on their own personal journeys, in this lifetime. This was the start for me. This is where the divine light from within me started to shine.

I still had a lot of work to do and many more regressions to get me to the point of being totally free, into a place where I believed in my destiny as a spiritual warrior, placed here on Planet Earth to help inspire and motivate others to succeed in their own lives.

Now I live my life day in, day out wanting to reach out to as many human beings as possible. I live to motivate and fill others' hearts with joy and happiness, whilst maintaining a deep and profound sense of love and gratefulness for my own life and that of my family's. Remember we have to love ourselves first and foremost before we can go out into the world and truly help other people. We need to fill ourselves up with so much love that it spills out into the lives of others. You too, very soon, will be in the same boat as me, loving yourself for who you are and appreciating this golden opportunity you have to make a difference to this planet we live on.

It's time to release the spiritual warrior within you. It all starts with love.

Meeting James

*Those who bring sunshine into the lives of
others cannot keep it from themselves.*

– J.M.Barrie, *nineteenth-century Scottish novelist*

Each and every one of us is pure on the inside and angels and beings
of divine light, who are here to bring peace and harmony to our
planet, only see the good in all of us.

They see beyond the misdemeanour of our current existence and
help us portray an image of true delight, that which we all long for,
but think is too hard to reach. If they or any of us focus on the inner
being that lies within us all, we can bring that special, kind and caring
being to the surface to flourish. Our time here on Mother Earth can
be so special. Mother Earth herself is so special and the very fact that
we connect and feel her every thought and beat of motion, allows us
to be a part of this magical zest fest, here on our planet.

Every single one of us has guides and when you start to become
aware they will appear, either in your mind's eye or sometimes in
the physical or sometimes both. Quite often I will see them half and
half. I have several guides that are with me constantly and the first of
these guides that I met was an elderly man called James.

Up until meeting James, I had been able to see very clearly during
my regressions but could not see any auras around people's bodies,
spirits or guides. In a way, I was jealous of people that could.
Jealousy is not a good emotion but I was still on a path of cleansing
and understanding. I won't say learning because I am still learning
now. We all learn each and every day and those that think they have

nothing to learn need to harness that ego and take control of their lives.

In 2006 two of my friends and I went to a meeting at a man's house, near Guildford in Surrey. It was an open invite to anyone who wanted to come and learn about 2012 and the end of the Mayan calendar. As my friends and I were starting our spiritual journey, we were very intrigued and wanted to find out and absorb as much information as we could.

We went to a small cottage around seven o'clock in the evening and there were several people there, all from different walks of life and the host of this gathering was a man called Tony. That's not his real name but I will call him Tony for the sake of this story.

The décor in the house was very dated and most of the others who attended were at least fifty years of age. We were all in our mid-twenties. The atmosphere in the house was very easy and we listened as Tony talked, hoping to enlighten us.

Something very strange happened. He came to me and was talking to me and I posed a question that contradicted what he had just said. I wasn't trying to annoy him but it was said out of pure curiosity. He stopped and stared at me for what seemed like an eternity and as he did his face changed shape and I saw what looked like a reptilian come through and take over his face. It was a funny shade of green and he held his stare with me, looking right into my eyes and it seemed like he was trying to use some sort of mind control over me.

I felt very uncomfortable and then he changed and looked normal again and carried on speaking. My friends and I stayed until the end of the night and all drove back together afterwards. They said they saw his face change too, and it was very creepy.

When my friend Tommy arrived at his home, he got out of his car. He said he felt like someone was behind him and when he turned around nothing was there, but he could feel the breath on his neck. I didn't find this out until the next morning.

When I arrived home it was about 11pm and I took a shower, thinking about what had happened. I was thinking away and then I saw a picture of a man in my mind and he spoke to me. He asked if I was OK. He said he was there to look after me, due to the experience earlier on and that the man was not happy with me and that he was trying to use his mind to interfere with mine and my friends.

I asked, 'Who are you?' 'James,' he replied. I said, 'Are you alive?' He said, 'I am a guide or angel as you may call me and I am here to protect you and guide you from here on in.' I talked to James for about ten minutes in the shower. The picture in my mind was so vivid, it was surreal. I kept shaking my head to see if he would go, but he remained constant.

I got out of the shower, dressed and went downstairs. I lay on the sofa, got comfy and continued my dialogue with James. We talked for over an hour and it was if he were actually there with me in the room. It was amazing. He explained that he would be with me now, as a constant companion and I could ask him advice, questions or whatever I needed to ask, at any time.

In the end I went up to bed and fell asleep. I had the deepest sleep ever.

The next morning I met my friend Tommy and we exchanged our stories. Something else happened to me that day: I started seeing everyone's auras. It was as though something had happened the night before that heightened all of my feelings and raised my awareness and now I could see much clearer, on many different levels. The

auras on some people were quite overwhelming and very off-putting.
I suppose because I hadn't experienced it before; it was totally new.

I phoned Trish, from the Tree of Life Centre, and explained what
had happened. She did some remote clearing for me and calmed me
down and gave me some affirmations to do. I was excited, felt strange
and was totally blown away all at once. I had, in my mind, gone up
a level on my journey. I had always wanted to see auras and now I
could.

Having James by my side was great; I felt deep comfort and trusted
him immensely. At first I was communicating nonstop. I was like
a little kid with a new toy, not being able to put it down. I thought
to myself, am I annoying him? No was the answer I received back
before I even finished my sentence. It was like he knew what I was
about to think before I even thought it. How amazing.

James explained to me that he did not judge me or worry about what
I had or hadn't done. He was simply there to observe, guide and
balance where possible, to aid me on my own personal journey.

After this revelation I started seeing other people's guides too. When
I was walking my daughter Aalayah to school in the mornings, I
could see this beautiful, ethereal like lady, in a white, long, silky
gown walking behind her. 'I am here to watch over her,' she told me.
It was amazing; there we were at 9 in the morning, walking along a
busy, leafy street in Richmond, Surrey and there was Aalayah and me
and this incredible presence of a woman walking behind us. It was
amazing. I was getting more and more excited. I couldn't wait to get
home and tell my wife.

Rest of the Team

If the only prayer you said in your whole life
was "Thank you", that would suffice.

– Meister Eckhart, *thirteenth-century German theologian*

All of us have many light beings, guides, angels; regardless of the terminology, they are all much the same, protectors, and beings of divine light from heaven, looking after, guiding and protecting the souls that need their help on this dense planet.

As I continued to see Trish and go into more and more past lives, understanding myself more and more on a daily basis, I grew in character and emotional strength. I gradually started to understand myself more and more as the weeks went by, and started to feel more comfortable about myself and who I was.

When I first realised this, I actually became comfortable in this new-found belief in myself. I wanted to share it with the world. Everyone I engaged in conversation with, friends, family, total strangers – it didn't matter who it was – I told them what I had experienced and what I now believed in. I told everyone I met that we are souls living in a vessel that is carrying us here on Planet Earth and that we have had a large number of past life experiences on this earth plane, and many other dimensions also. I told people about James and that we spoke constantly.

A lot of people looked at me as though I was plain nuts and looked around as if to see where the men and women in white coats were... how did I get out? Others listened, just out of politeness and some were receptive to the notion of a much larger and exciting Universe.

I learned after a while that I needed to pick and choose who I spoke to about this subject. I quickly worked out who were the right candidates or not. The ones that weren't I always tried to find a subtle way of saying you know what, we have all had an average of approximately seven hundred and fifty past lives, what do you think of that? Can you see James? Look, he's standing right next to me. Well actually I could never find a subtle way so either just came out with it or left the subject well alone. It took many funny looks before I got the message. I am smiling right now writing this, thinking about some of the facial expressions people gave me.

As I continued with my regressions and furthermore peeled away the layers of the onion I met more and more guides on my travels that ended up staying with me. The next was Layla. Layla was a woman who looked like she was in her late twenties, with long blonde-locked hair and a white satin dress. She was very kind and spoke with a soft voice.

After Layla I met Tenan, an Indian chief who gave me snake medicine used for healing. Tenan was an elderly gentleman and he was smoking a peace pipe when I met him travelling through a past life where I too was an American Indian, living on a reservation. I was a leader and a warrior and carried many of my people into battle to fight for our freedom. I had a picture of Tenan tattooed on my side and a snake also to represent the medicine he gave me. He speaks with authority and is quick to let me know when I have strayed off my path.

The last of my guides who is there with me constantly is Cruso, a Portuguese warrior that always stands to the left and behind me slightly. He is enormous, about 7ft tall, and weighs in at about 180kgs of solid muscle. He has been with me through many lifetimes and has protected me in many times of strife. Cruso has a great personality, as do my other light beings, but Cruso has a good sense of humour. He will be sarcastic at times and brutally honest. If I make a mistake and he believes I have not learned my lesson, then he will be the first one to pull me aside, and let me know how he feels.

Between James, Layla, Tenan and Cruso there is not much that can't be answered or solved. I am very lucky to have such awesome guides. As a light worker here on Earth these guys have helped me tremendously on my journey back to the light, from the not-so-light place I once spent my time, to the peaceful place in my heart that I now choose to live. The great thing is with your guides they never judge you. I have done some silly things before I was fully immersed back in the light and not once did any of them judge me. They just discussed it with me and guided me back on track.

That's one thing that us humans here on Earth have to deal with, is feelings. Happiness, sadness, joy, grief, smiles and anger. On higher, lighter vibrating levels of consciousness the beings there are not burdened with these emotions. All they feel is pure love. It is special there and souls at the source just go about their daily tasks just getting on with the mission at hand. They are never sucked into arguments, issues or problems; they do not exist on other planes. Only here on Earth is the energy dense and does darkness live.

Actually it's not darkness. It's just a lack of light due to the dense, energetic cycle that relishes and tries to control us. The lack of light causes a lack of love and purity and this lack of love and purity can cause ill feelings such as hatred, jealousy or anger, emotions that are unknown as you raise your spiritual vibration.

If it's so good when we are happy, feeling proud and joyous, why not work on yourself and discover ways in which you can make yourself feel happy, joyous and proud of who you are at all times? It does take practice, constant practice, every day. It has to be a part of your daily routine to work on your mind, body and soul and find peace in your heart.

Just as one would go to the gym and train their bodies and muscles to grow and become stronger so must you train the spiritual aspect of your being. If you undertake physical exercise for one year and then stop for a few weeks, you lose a large percentage of what you have gained. The same goes for the spiritual aspect of your mind, body and soul. It must be trained. Coming from a dense place with a lack of light and holding yourself in this new space of profound happiness and gratitude, takes practice but the effort that's necessary is worth it. The mental effort required is priceless. The comparison between the place of lack of light and the place of light and the effort that has to be generated to bridge the gap is seemingly negligible. Once you are in your place of Zen, you will not want to go back, ever.

Once you arrive at this new found place of happiness and delight, at your very existence on this beautiful planet you will find others, who haven't travelled your road as of yet, wanting to pull you back down to their dense and unlit world. You just have to remain focused, continue to love yourself and shine love into the lives of others around you. That is how we, as a global community, will raise the global vibration here on Planet Earth. Firstly you need to play your part and raise your consciousness, and then you need to let your new-found light heighten your experience and you will become a walking, talking beacon of positive energy, affecting all with whom you come in contact with energetically.

You will not need to communicate with people verbally and tell them what you have accomplished. You can if you want; however, your presence on Earth, with your new vibration, will be enough to have a huge positive effect. Join me and many others who are walking the walk right now. I can sense your divine light bursting inside of you, wanting to shine brighter and brighter and join the party.

It's warm and cosy in here. Open the door and come on in. You are more than welcome. In fact your invitation went out years ago and finally you have decided to take action and follow your instincts, which lead you to this book. It's time for you to step into the light and join your fellow spiritual warriors, on our quest to bring peace, joy and happiness to our world.

There are many other planets that require the stability and peace on Mother Earth to prevail, so other planets within our solar system are not affected. We have to bring Mother Earth back into balance. Now is the time. I look forward to seeing you on the other side and working with you in harmony.

2012 – The End

What a wonderful life I'd had! I only wish I'd realised it sooner.

– Colette, *Twentieth-century French novelist*

In 2006, I was shown a future map of the world. It was drawn from visions and created by the Matrix Institute in America. It was all about the end of the Earth as we know it. It showed much of Europe and America under water and new lands that had risen once again, such as Atlantis and Lemuria. Many of you may have seen this map.

As I had started this new journey, my spiritual journey, at the time I very much had a strong sense that I needed to move to New Zealand, where the map showed that the land mass had increased. It looked like a safe place for me to take my family and start a new life if England was to be under water.

So in 2009 I moved my family to New Zealand and we set up a health and fitness centre. We moved to Napier on the east coast of the North Island. It was a great place for Laura, the kids and me, and we were very happy.

We believed that these shifts in the Earth were going to take place (like many other people) and that there would be mass flooding but they never came. Twenty-twelve came and went and nothing had happened. It's now April 2013 as I am writing this and it's only recently that I understand why we went to New Zealand. It wasn't to escape mass flooding and starvation; it was to grow spiritually. Both my wife and I and our children all grew in different ways, from going to New Zealand, and living there. Everything always works out perfectly if you trust and accept that life is giving you exactly what you need at this particular time in this particular space. All is always good in the Universe.

The Universe had given us the map. That was just a catalyst to make us go. The real work was to be done when we arrived. Before we all went to New Zealand we were very much living a life that wasn't real. It was real at the time for our current situation but it was not who we were or what we were supposed to be doing. My wife and children grew in many ways. My wife became more confident and really found herself. She learned to teach Yoga and became a very good Yoga teacher at our gym. She blossomed in New Zealand and she started to grow and, I believe, love herself unconditionally, for the first time in her life. Both of my children were allowed to be free spirits for the first time in their lives and they came into their own and were living in their element.

I also found myself. When we went to New Zealand we planned on starting an eco-building project as you know. It was going very well. We had all the plans drawn up and I flew my UK partners out to NZ for a presentation. The local council agreed to give us planning permission and everything was a green light and then out of nowhere the deal fell apart at the seams due to some unforeseen circumstances involving Maori land law.

The Universe and my guides were working in unison to orchestrate this. I was gutted at the time but after realising the grand scheme of things, and why it happened, now I look back and smile.

I had no money so knew I had to go to work. I started a personal training/fitness business and rented some space in another gym. I started doing very well and built up a great client base. After several months the gym owner asked me for more money for my space as I was doing so well. I said no and so she asked me to leave her gym.

I thought to myself there is nowhere else that I could train as the rules were too strict and so I used all the money I had saved from eight months of personal training, working 5am to 10pm, 6 days a week, to fund and start my own gym. What this did was give me a platform. I was teaching classes and instructing large groups of people and my work became well recognised for the results my clients were achieving. This led to several television appearances on Good Morning TV. I was doing exercise routines for the viewers at home. My confidence grew and it also really cemented my eagerness to help others succeed in terms of health and fitness and, in turn, their daily lives.

I found that I became a magnet for people needing help and guidance physically, spiritually and mentally. If I had stayed and my eco business had become successful I may not have gone down this road. You see the Universe knew what I was supposed to be doing and so made sure my eco business failed and I had to find an alternative. I was being guided every step of the way. At the time it was hard and times were tough but I kept going and life worked out perfectly in the end.

We all have a true purpose. Every human being was created to fulfil a specific mission. We all have guides in the form of people, angels and circumstances that gently or sometimes harshly bring us back on track. Acceptance at every turn is the key. I had to accept my eco-building project falling apart and then the gym owner asking me to leave. At the time it seemed harsh but this was divine intervention guiding me to my life's purpose.

After having the gym for two years both my wife and I started to get itchy feet. We felt like we were supposed to do more. We had achieved all we could at this gym. You can only help so many people in a gym and on TV in New Zealand with its 4.5 million population; we wanted to motivate millions of people all over the world and were on the lookout for something else.

De-construct and Re-build

If you let go a little, you will have a little peace. If you let go a lot, you will have a lot of peace. If you let go completely, you will have complete peace.

– The Venerable Ajahn Chah, twentieth-century Buddhist monk

What I have noticed with myself and many others who are searching their souls for the answers and discovering the truth about who and what we really are, is that it's a process. A process that involves, quite often, one where an individual pulls him or herself apart and rebuilds.

What each and every one of us human beings has, is a solid foundation, just like that of a house that needs rebuilding. A dilapidated house that is in need of much love and attention, has often gotten in such a state that it has to be gutted inside and then put back together again. When it comes to a house the foundation and the framework is often sound, it's just the walls and the interior that are rotten or windows that may be mouldy and falling apart. Or maybe a new roof must be assembled.

A human being that has drifted off track and has been led astray by the ego and the density of this planet, still has a body and a soul and that inner spark of light never ever totally goes out. So just like the house is left with its solid foundation and framework, so is the human being left with its bodily structure and soul.

Through constant daily effort of channelling your thoughts and tasks in the right direction, one can de-construct and re-build themselves into the man or woman that was sent to this planet to fulfil their mission. Some of us stay in the undesirable state, of being alive and controlled by this dense nature all of our lives, but we all have the opportunity to break free. It's up to the individual in question, whether or not they are prepared to put forth the necessary effort, and are willing to go through the sometimes lengthy de-construction process, to enable them to strip away all the unsavoury benefits instilled into us humans. I want you to know that the process of enlightenment can often happen instantaneously. For me it took time but I know others who have found peace very quickly.

Many opportunities are offered to each and every one of us and it's a choice if we take them or not. There is never any pressure; if you choose not to then not one being of divine light will criticise or have ill feelings towards you. Why? The reason is simple. Beings of divine light do not judge. They see each and every one of us as perfection and they also know how difficult it can be, here on this planet, living in this time and space with the negativity that surrounds us daily. They know how influential the media and the world news systems are, and that their protocol of feeding our minds with numbing material on a consistent basis, has a prolific effect on our thoughts and actions.

It is up to you, what you decide to do. My advice is to listen to your heart and not to your head. Your head, your conscious mind will see the necessary effort required as laborious and draining and not worth it in the end. It will also have the ego nagging away, telling it this and that and keeping you in a state of fear, wherever it can.

Your heart will tell you otherwise and if you ask your heart, by posing questions, it will respond and guide you. If you hand yourself over to the Universe and your guides they will ensure that you take the right path. They will give you small signs and if you relax your mind and listen you will either hear or see them and your life will magically start to change. This is my promise to you.

2012 – The Beginning

We are disturbed not by what happens to us, but
by our thoughts about what happens.

– Epictetus

My wife and I were thinking we needed to do something else, other than the gym work, to help humanity but did not know what. It just felt like we should and then the signs got stronger and stronger.

When I moved to New Zealand with Laura and the children we planned, as you know, on setting up an eco-housing project. It had been our plan from day one. We entered New Zealand on a three year working visa. What that meant was that in order to obtain permanent residency we would have to prove that in three years' time we had properly established our company, undertaken our first project, employed local people and were making a profit and paying taxes.

Of course none of this happened as the business did not go ahead. So we started the gym. The problem was that we started the gym and didn't tell anyone. I went to see a local visa counsellor who has never lost a case in getting visas agreed for British residents in New Zealand, and he has dealt with cases much harder than ours. Ours, in his eyes, was very simple.

We started the gym at the beginning of 2011 and it went very well. We employed people and had a number of local gym contractors running our classes, built a fantastic reputation, made money, paid our taxes and everything looked very promising. When I went to see Ron, our local visa specialist, he told me we would apply for a three year working visa under Laura's name and then go for permanent residency, very soon, as the gym had already been going for a year and a half when I went to see him.

We went through the motions, did all our medicals, paid our fees, filled out all our forms and sent them off. They came back and declined our visas for two reasons. Reason number one: we didn't tell them we were setting the business up; and reason two: our cash flow projections were not feasible. These were cash flow projections that Ron himself put together for us that were based on our last one and a half years' trading. It was nonsense.

So we appealed and they agreed that the cash flows were OK and got over the fact that we didn't tell them we were starting it. Next they declined us for another reason, a reason that they didn't mention the first time around. They said that Laura didn't have the experience to be running a business and that I was not a bona fide applicant as I already had a business visa for my eco project and that I should not be working in the gym.

Was the Universe telling us something? Jerry and Laura, you have other work to do, please leave this country and go and do it. At first we didn't cotton on to what was happening; we just couldn't believe they wouldn't let us stay.

So we appealed a third time and then we twigged. We sat down and just looked at each other and laughed. We are fighting against this and giving all the correct answers to win our case but still the Universe is saying no. It was at this point we realised we had to go somewhere. But where?

We had pulled our fairy cards several months earlier. You pick three cards from a deck and they represent past, present and future. The cards back then made little sense but now, being in the present situation we were in, made perfect sense. The holiday that our fairy cards had predicted came about.

We knew we had a greater purpose and were prepared to go forth but were unsure as to what that purpose was. We decided to go on holiday and take some time to relax and think. We booked a relaxing holiday on Moorea, a small island next to Tahiti.

So we booked our tickets and flew from Napier to Auckland to get our connecting flight to Tahiti. When we arrived at the airport we checked in and went through to the departure lounge. Our plane was called and we went up to the gate. Whilst we were waiting an announcement came over the tannoy and we were told our plane was delayed, and would be an hour or so.

Now, leading up to this holiday I had had several messages from the Universe and my guides to re-read a book I had read many times before, but didn't respond. I kept making excuses and you should never do that when the Universe is calling out to you. This particular book is called The Science Of Getting Rich, by Wallace Wattles – an amazing book about creating a rich life for yourself. I had read it hundreds of times, maybe nigh on a thousand, since I bought it, in 2006, in Auckland when we were waiting for our plane. Coincidence?

So the immediate thought that entered my mind when the plane was delayed was that book. It flashed in my mind and I knew this was a strong sign from the Universe that I had to listen. It had held up a plane full of passengers after all, just so that I could read this book and get the end of the message. I picked it up and read for a few minutes. My whole life just flashed in front of my eyes like a video reel on fast forward, flying though my life and little snippets really stood out and slapped me around the face.

I looked up at Laura who was sat opposite me and I said, 'I have to write a book. I have to write a book on my life to inspire people.' It was so strong, the feeling inside, and so directed, that I knew this was my mission. But I have never written before, I thought, this should be interesting. However, in my heart of hearts, I just knew it would be perfect.

Understanding Jerry Sargeant

*There is only one cause of unhappiness; the false beliefs
you have in your head, beliefs so wide spread, so commonly
held, that it never occurs to you to question them.*

– Anthony de Mello, *Jesuit priest and psychotherapist*

All the past life regression therapy I had done and all the hard work
I had put in to developing me as a human being was immense. I
knew that I had evolved spiritually in many ways. It wasn't until I
started writing, however, that I really understood myself and my life's
purpose.

The last seven years of my life had been a constant build up to me
realising and understanding myself. Actually it was more than seven
years. It was more like 12 years because that's when I first met Laura,
back in Spain, all those years ago. It was Laura who rescued me from
my drink and drug fuelled benders and gave me the most precious
gift a woman could give a man, apart from eternal love.

That was the gift of our very first child. It was at this moment, having
Laura and Aalayah in my life, that the changes started to happen
and it was an ever increasing work in progress to make me into the
human being that I am today. When I think about it hard it has been
a thirteen year battle of emotions to understand who Jerry Sargeant
really is. Step by step, piece by piece, I de-constructed my make-up
and re-built myself from the inside out. Not on my own of course.
The support of Laura and her strong willpower gave me the boost
and support I needed to take action. Stopping drinking and partying
was the first port of call.

Discovering the angry old man was next and that set me on my spiritual journey at The Tree Of Life Centre and I met Trish, an angel sent from heaven. Undergoing the past life regression was an integral part of the journey and during this period I had been drawn to New Zealand. Laura, the children and I started getting our visas for NZ before we even travelled there. It just felt right.

Going to NZ under false pretences from the Universe to start an eco-project was perfection. A gymnasium would not have made me excited, but the thought of helping the environment did. Little did I know when our project was no more, that an even greater mission for us to embark on would be presented. Running the gym and going on television made me come out into the public arena and feel comfortable there. This was just the prelude, the birthing process of the Universe preparing Jerry Sargeant, the light worker, for his real mission: the mission to go out and publicly lay his heart on the table and bare all to the world. Letting the world know what I have discovered. Motivating and inspiring the human race to wake up, and take action to help save our planet.

This was my real mission from the moment I incarnated into this body. To stand up and be counted. To rise up and stand in front of millions of people and tell them the truth, knowing that I could be ridiculed and ostracised for doing so. Does it bother me? No it doesn't because I know this is utter perfection. This is exactly what I am supposed to be doing. Nothing in my life, apart from meeting Laura, a beautiful Romanian girl, has ever felt so perfect.

When I started to write my books it was so surreal. It was like I was not even writing them. I was like a PA, sat at my computer, writing for the Universe and the greater good of the human race. I did not think once. It just flowed out of me and my first book The Magnet & the Genie 'Maximum Wealth' was created. It was the first of three books to be written in the Magnet & the Genie Trilogy. Maximum

Health has been finished and is waiting to be sent to the publishers as I am writing this. I was about to write Maximum Love when I was out jogging on a Sunday morning and saw some fairies buzzing around an old tree. I connected with them instantly then an angel appeared in front of me. He told me his name was Archangel Gabriel and I was told to leave aside Maximum Love and write 'Into the Light' – Raising the Global Vibration first, this very book you are reading now.

When Gabriel appeared in front of me he was very tall. Maybe 7 feet. His body was ethereal like but as real as you looking at the pages in this book. He looked strong and noble, and spoke with authority but with kindness and gentleness at the same time. I have come to realise that communication with infinite intelligence, angels, fairies and other beings of light requires a deep trust. The human rational thinking mind cannot comprehend what you see or hear so your ego will always try and configure doubt within your mind.

I travelled back to New Zealand a few months ago and had confirmation from the Universe that I was on the perfect path. Not that I had doubted for a second but it's always nice to receive added confirmation from the Universe. I was inside a crystal shop with my family and I had this strong sense to ask the lady if they sold any books on angels. She directed me to a corner of the shop and a particular book caught my eye. My eyes were drawn to it like a magnet. I picked it up and opened the page. Which page in the book do you think it opened on? That's right: Archangel Gabriel. Is that coincidence? Maybe. You have to ask yourself though out of the hundreds of angels in the book I opened it on the very page of the Angel that has been guiding me. Coincidence or confirmation? I smiled from ear to ear and a deep sense of calmness filled my body.

The information in this book is totally channelled information. Valuable knowledge and experience that higher guardians of this realm feel human beings, just like you, need to know and hear. Some people ask how do you know you are not writing this and you are being guided? Well to me it's so clear. I don't actually talk or write in the way that some of this book is written. When I look back at it I am surprised that some of this actually came from me.

You see, within the invisible realms of space and love lies a Universal Database of knowledge and wisdom. It's been there since the dawn of time and is readily available for everyone to access. Create the space in your life and I promise you out from that space will flow the answers to all of your questions. Out from that space will flow your true purpose, your Universal mission, the misison you chose as a being of light before embarking on your earthly journey and this beautiful human experience.

My heart is beaming with glorious joy.

Don't ask for Our Help Again

The mind is its own place, and in itself can make a Heaven of Hell, a Hell of Heaven.

– **John Milton,** *English poet*

There was one telling moment during all of my regressions when I knew I had turned a point. A place in my mind, body and soul that enabled me to continue on my journey in peace.

It was this moment that I had been working myself up to. I didn't know how or when it would come but I knew there would be a turning point when I would have stripped my last piece of darkness away, and discarded it from my soul. My light energy that no longer needed any shape or form of darkness wrapped around it any more.

I was sat in the chair opposite Trish again – I lost count how many times after a few hundred. They all seemed to blur into one and I really had to connect to differentiate between them all. It was a late evening around 8 o'clock that I sat down in Trish's chair. Both of us knew subconsciously that this particular session was going to be a rougher ride than usual. Over time, we were going into the dark layers around the core of my soul, and they were getting harder and harder to release.

We went through our normal ritual of seeing my golden bubble come around my chair, to walking through the smile and into the field, to finding my tree and embracing Mother Earth and Father Sky once more.

We went down to a level that connected me to a part of my life shortly after my birth into this body and it was mind blowing to see how much of an effect my fostering and adoption process had affected me and the fact that I was taken from my birth mother and into another room, without any connection or loving bond being allowed. My mother was mistreated, mentally and physically, and it had had a huge effect on us both.

Shortly after being in this old world I drifted through time and space and came back into a room where I found myself looking at what seemed like a chastised prison victim, crunched and humbled on the floor. It was the aspect of my soul in that lifetime. He was withdrawn and skinny and undernourished, shackled in chains. I walked over and spoke to him with the intention of releasing him and turning him into light and positivity and to set him free, knowing that I was the future progression of his soul and that all was OK. I was in safe hands and learning to live a life of freedom, where I loved unconditionally, both myself and the rest of humanity.

As we spoke he turned to face me and I could see the torment and guilt in his face. All he wanted to do was to be free and to move on. At present he was stuck, and my duty was to let him be free and stop the suffering.

As I leant forward to embrace him and bring him home I became aware of the room Trish and I were sat in.

I sat with my eyes wide open and could see Trish looking at me two metres away in the opposite chair. What happened next is ingrained into my memory like it was yesterday.

As we looked at each other a mist appeared inside the room, making our visibility less clear. It was like we were in a thick fog but inside the room. This wasn't something Trish or I saw with our mind's eye but our real eyes; the room went cold also. Trish and I were looking at each other and then to my left and Trish's right a man of about 30 years of age walked through the wall and into the room. He was a businessman and had come to negotiate an important deal. For him it was probably a regular occurrence but for me it was a first and a last and something very unusual, but at the same time feeling so right.

He was wearing a brown suit, carrying a leather briefcase and his hair was well groomed and swept immaculately to the left hand side. He walked boldly into the room and looked down to his right where I was placed in the chair. I say placed as I wasn't sat. My whole body throughout the last twenty to thirty minutes had started to seize up. I felt like a disabled human being, hunched up in my chair. My arms and hands had curled inwards and I had extreme tension and stiffness in my body, and no control over it, much like the chastised prison victim, the aspect of my soul I had seen minutes earlier.

When he turned and looked at me I had to use every morsel of energy within my entire being to turn my head about three centimetres to the left, so I could look up out of the corner of my eyes and see him.

This was the moment that all my past life regressions had led to. It was the defining moment, where I would rid myself of any dark elements left clinging to my soul. I was about to sign the final and inevitable contract that would change my life forever. The man looked at me and said, 'Jerry, if you make this decision you can never ask for our help again. Are you sure you want to do this?'

It was the strangest feeling ever. For me to say yes, it was extremely hard. I wanted to so much but it was like I was paralysed and unable to speak, similar to losing the power of speech after a temporary brain injury I had sustained at boxing shortly before.

I looked up, my body crippled in a way I cannot even describe by this point. It was like I had to push my head through metal to look at him, a solid steel door. That was the amount of effort it took for me to turn further towards him and then finally say, 'yes I am sure'.

He asked me one further time, 'Are you sure that this is what you want?' 'Yes,' I replied. 'OK,' he said, 'fair enough,' and he turned and walked back through the wall. He was gone. The mist started to clear in the room and my body started to release. I was left slumped in the chair with zero energy. Almost lifeless but high as a kite at the same time as I had accomplished my mission. Trish looked at me and said, 'well done, my love' – it was so surreal.

Did that really just happen, I thought to myself?

At this time I was involved in a deal which would have netted me millions of pounds and at the last minute it fell apart at the seams for no apparent reason. It wasn't until a year or so later when I was driving along in my car that it came to me. Of course it fell apart at the seams. I had agreed I did not want their help any more so why would the deal have worked out? It was a dodgy deal after all. Ever since that day I have lived a different life, one full of honesty, peace, love and pure happiness and I am so, so grateful.

Love always dissolves any negative forces. Light always prevails over darkness. Love and light are the keys to a harmonious world where the planet's resources have been shared equally between all men, women and children. Love is the doorway to heaven.

The Birth Process

We can never obtain peace in our outer world
until we make peace with ourselves.

– His Holiness the Dalai Lama

During the incident mentioned in the previous chapter, I discovered
all about the birthing process and how much it affects children,
if things don't go according to plan – and also when they do go
according to plan.

As a child I was off the charts in terms of my behaviour. My parents
could never work me out and I was always in trouble at school, with
the police, neighbours. You name it: I had pretty much done it.

When a baby is born it has usually spent nine months in the womb
connected to its mother and a strong bond is created. If a baby is
born and is taken away from its mother, without being allowed to
spend that quality time resting in her arms, continuing that special,
loving bond, something is lost – that connection, the feeling of being
wanted and loved – and the child, without wanting to, will feel a
disconnection from day one on entering this world.

Now let me give you another scenario, one that I experienced and
many of you will have also. My mother decided that although she
would give birth to me she also knew when she was just two or three
months pregnant that she would let me go once I was born, not
because she really wanted to but because she thought she would not
be able to bring me up on her own with the current conditions of life
she was living in. So, emotionally as a baby in my mother's womb I
would have felt a lack of love and abandonment. I would have felt a

number of mixed up emotions that would have started to condition me before I was even born.

Later in my life, for many years I suffered with rejection issues. Speaking on stage at live events took a long time for me to become comfortable with as I was always battling with the fear of being rejected.

There are many babies and children that endure this process and enter the world having had their emotions spun around in a high speed washing machine, not really knowing whether they are coming or going. Often these children grow into teenagers and then adults and throughout their lives struggle within their relationships because the emotional scars of rejection or abandonment have instilled fear into them. This fear creates a sense that they will be abandoned again by another human being and so often the man or woman in question may create a situation which will cause the pain to be felt all over again. Often marriages break down because of this reason. A pattern that was instilled before the child was even born travelled into adult life with them and caused suffering once more. This happens a lot of the time and the sad thing is that these patterns are created when we don't have a choice or are totally unaware.

It's a choice as spirit, when sitting on our cloud, we choose to make. After incarnating, however, we forget this and have to, as a baby and then a young child growing up, find ourselves again. This can take some time. Some of us, who suffer this trauma at birth, never really get over it or understand why we feel pain or hatred as a youngster and just want to cause chaos and harm.

I am reaching out right now to any men or women who may have been fostered or adopted and lost that connection with their mothers at birth. Maybe it will give you an idea of why you may have felt a disconnection to life through this bodily experience here on Planet

Earth. It's only us human beings that suffer this kind of pain. Other levels on the astral playing field are different; love and emotions are appeased.

I am hoping you can find peace in your hearts, even at a later stage in your lives. I know this message will find so many of you as I am being directed to write it. You are truly amazing and maybe this has been a block in your life that has stopped you from discovering your true potential. Some people live and die and never truly understand themselves, and/or learn the lessons here on Earth that they were supposed to learn, so inevitably will have to come back and learn it all over again, in the next bodily experience.

That's what this life is after all, a training exercise and Earth is our training ground. We are like a huge football team trying to live amongst each other and train, understand and eventually learn to become a part of a fluent and flawless team, ready to go on and achieve the highest of heights on this motherly realm.

I also want everyone who has been born to know, even those who have not been separated from their birth mother: the birthing process itself is quite traumatic for a small baby. Think about it: not many women have natural births, without the use of pain-killing drugs. If the pain is eased of a full grown woman, think about what effect the drugs will have on a tiny baby. The baby comes out, off his or her head. High as a kite, that's the reality of the situation, so the birth process is traumatic for any baby. This is worth knowing.

I applaud every one of you who is reading this right now and soaking up this intended knowledge. Many of us light workers have sacrificed ourselves to enable this knowledge and wisdom to be realised and brought to the forefront of the human experience, so you can gain from these valuable lessons and use them to find your heart, and love yourself from within. Learn to love yourself unconditionally, every part of you from the inside out, regardless of your start in life; love yourself eternally as you are truly amazing. A special soul with a special purpose.

You are a divine being of light, just like I am and just like the rest of our brotherly and sisterly friends among this vast, multi-cultural human race. We are one, originating from one divine source and at this time of evolution are being brought back to that special place once again where we will all reunite, in perfect harmony with nature and Mother Earth herself.

We are all guided along our journeys and some of us realise and become aware of this help. Others carry on and then more help is given and more of us wake up. Help will continue to be given to us until each and every human being wakes up and rises out into the light. That day will be a special moment, one to rejoice in and feel the ecstasy as we give birth again to an avalanche of love and light.

If you can imagine that when you are born you are pure and full of love and as you grow and experience life you are taken on an emotional roller coaster, one that covers you in layers and layers of different negative emotions such as anger, hurt, resentment, jealousy, fear of loss, fear of rejection, lack of love and a number of other emotions that turn into personal baggage that we carry around with us on our journey. It's no wonder that in carrying the intensity of some of our experiences we get weighed down and the events we go through instil disempowering beliefs into us that cause destructive behavioural patterns that do not serve us.

We end up cloaked in layers and layers of emotional baggage and it stops us seeing the light.

If you can imagine a picture of a human being in a heart. That's you. Now imagine 10 to 15 layers of emotions around you. It could be more or less. You're like the centre piece of an onion and the layers travel out and get bigger and bigger.

Now picture another human being on the outside of all of these layers. That's you again looking back in at the you on the inside, the one surrounded in a bubble of light. You know you can get back to that place and rediscover the purity, love and light once more. To do it you need to peel away the layers of the onion, stripping away the emotions and as you do you shred the experience and as the light pours back into your life it gets stronger and brighter. The more layers you strip away the brighter you get and the lighter and more vibrant you feel. When you reach the middle you will be in a total state of harmony, connected to source once more, enlightened. This is the light we are travelling towards. This is the light that is within us all and that never goes out. This is the light that graces our planet and fills the entire Universe with love, light and compassion. This is the light that lives forever inside every human being on this planet.

This is the light that embraces humanity and burns forever in the hearts of the global community we are creating.

Yin and Yang

The best years of your life are the ones in which you decide your problems are your own. You do not blame them on your mother, the ecology, or the president. You realise that you control your own destiny.

– Dr Albert Ellis, *psychologist*

When I think with my logical mind, this chapter should have been written earlier on but I am being told no, this is the perfect order. Please just write for us, these messages must be passed.

If there is light there is dark; wherever there is suffering there is happiness. Wherever there is Yin there is Yang. Or is this the case?

I don't see that there is darkness and light although I have referred to darkness earlier in this book. There is more so light and a lack of light. There is love and a lack of love. The other emotions that are a lack of love such as anger and hatred can be easily remedied by adding more love to the equation.

Add more love to the cake of life that you are baking, and the results will be a fluffy, light, refreshing and tasty cake that will melt in your mouth. A cake made with a lack of love, care and attention will not cook correctly and the final presentation will look and taste much the same; the lack of effort and consequently love, will have uncelebrated the final presentation.

You must look for the love in all things; all creatures great and small must be loved. No one should be judged or an opinion formed without proper connection and even then after an inwardly connection, no man, woman or other living form should be judged under any circumstances. Each and every human being, animal, tree or being containing the force of life, should be met with a smile. The life force that is in every tree, plant and animal is the same life force that is within you and me.

We should always treat others equally and the same goes for the trees, plants and animals. We must take care of Mother Earth and all of her inhabitants, with a purity and cleanliness of that which you would take care of your own home.

You and I have feelings and every other living thing that is alive, with the formidable life force that is breathing deep inside us, and every other living thing has feelings too. You must respect this. Just as fellow human beings must be respected. If you are treated unfairly by another soul on this planet it does not make you feel very nice does it? It lowers your self-esteem when you are not on the universal vibration that you are moving towards and your day can be knocked out of shape.

Constant and relentless not so good feelings being pushed in your direction have the potential to knock your life right out of shape. Let's work together to ensure that every action and event that takes place in each of our own personal lives is performed with love and light and the betterment of humanity, our passionate motivator.

Let's care for one another with a relentless will to end the suffering here on Planet Earth. Let's unite, join forces and speed up the awakening of the world. Every day that you spend with your vibration aloft you will be like a powerful beacon of light, dancing in the moon and splashing in the ocean's waves, filling the world and its inhabitants with hope and lighting the pathway for others to follow.

Romania

*If you don't like something change it. If you can't
change it, change your attitude. Don't complain.*

– **Maya Angelou,** *author and poet*

Embarking on my spiritual journey was an enormous stepping stone
into the unknown. I ventured out of my comfort zone in a big way
until it became my new comfort zone, where I understood it and had
dissected it and become the man I am today.

There was one defining moment during my journey when I truly
understood the connection between the human body and the soul.
The human body after all is just a vessel that carries the soul on this
particular part of its journey. The body is the vessel that ensures the
soul can move through time and space on this particular escapade,
here on this planet.

In this lifetime, building up to my past life regression therapy and
the continuation of my mission, I had seen a number of dead bodies
– dead friends, family members or total strangers.

The universe, my Genie, gave me a chance to consider the human
body in much more detail and presented me with an event that
would make me see, in an instant, how the body and the soul are
two completely different elements that make up the human being. I
was shown that the human body, in all its glory really is just a vessel,
carrying this special life force on a magical journey, and when the
time came for the two to part company, I was there, in the thick of
the action, to see life for what it really is.

My family and I had gone back to visit my wife's family in Romania. We were in a taxi one morning driving from her town, Piatre Neamt, to Bucharest to catch a plane at the end of our stay. It was about four or five o'clock in the morning, it was still dark and we were travelling down a country road. I was in the passenger seat and Laura and the kids were in the back. This taxi had no seat belts in the back.

I was asleep in the passenger seat and then I heard a loud noise and woke up. All I could see was glass flying everywhere, my head was sore and there was wind coming through a hole in the windscreen. The car was swerving slightly and I felt disorientated.

I remember thinking to myself, we are in a serious accident and I thought we were going to hit the oncoming traffic on the other side of the road or maybe flip over. Then suddenly we came to a stop. It was so strange. I got out of the car, opened the back doors and Aalayah was on the floor under the driver's seat, Josh was in Laura's arms and both their mouths were full of glass. I looked back over the car and saw a lady who had been hit and her ankles smashed to bits and missing, with a second lady bent down looking after her.

I looked farther up the road and there seemed to be a body lying still on the ground. What had happened is that three women were crossing the road early in the morning to go to work. Our taxi had hit the first lady clean on, she had come through the windscreen, hit me in the head with her head and then got flipped over the car and landed one hundred metres up the road. The second lady tried to jump out the way and her ankles got caught as she tried to escape and the third lady was untouched.

As I proceeded to walk up the road it was such a surreal feeling. I knew she was dead. I walked up to the body, looked down and her body was totally mangled and lifeless. Her legs were wrapped up over her head and shoulder and she was in a real mess.

The strangest thing was that I looked at the body and saw that the soul had left immediately. It was like I was looking at a piece of rubbery plastic. I didn't look at her as a dead woman. All that stuck in my mind was this useless rubbery mess on the ground that the soul no longer had any use for. The soul had vacated and moved on within seconds. Just above the body, as I walked towards it, I saw the energy, the soul of the woman just hovering above the body. What was probably only a few seconds seemed like an eternity. This etheric, energetic, transparent substance hovered and then moved on, back to the spirit world, heaven or wherever it was travelling to next.

I looked up into the sky as the light was just coming through, took a deep breath of fresh morning air and then looked back down again and thanked the lady for this experience. I do not smoke but remember thinking to myself, a cigarette would just fit the moment perfectly. It was the kind of feeling you have when something amazing happens in your life and you want to celebrate.

I walked back to Laura and the kids and felt this sense of strange relief and joy at the same time. I had just discovered what happens after death, first hand, for the very first time and actually understood what had happened.

This may seem like odd behaviour to some people but at that very precise moment in time it all seemed utterly perfect. I really saw what life is. It's just a period of time whereby the soul, our soul, is in an earthly body, ready and willing to move on when the time is right. The soul has no love for the body; it's merely a vehicle the soul has to travel inside and when the time comes it goes back to source, to spirit, where it will continue its journey, a journey of continual growth and learning.

It's magnificent and as human beings we have nothing at all to fear of death. Life and death are perfect.

Bringing Back Your Power

Terror is the most modern weapon in the modern age and the western media is mercilessly using it against its own people.

– His Holiness the Dalai Lama

As you start to unravel the truth and realise who you are and what you are truly capable of, you will start to wake up and see certain elements of this world through a different pair of spectacles. One thing for me and many others that I know is the much needed feeling of owning a television and watching the garbage that is often pumped out through your screens.

Most of the information that we receive through our TV screens is mind numbing and really and truthfully, if you look at it carefully, pointless. The content we are shown is what I would call low vibrational or low frequency information, designed to subdue the masses. What use factor does it have on our lives? It just gives many human beings a chance to switch off and let their mind be absorbed into the horror transmitted by our world news stations. The fact of the matter is that we need to bring back our power and ensure that everything that goes into our minds is of a good and honest nature.

We want to put pure thoughts into our minds, images and material that will help us on our own personal quests. We need to unlock our heart and soul, and discover who we truly are and if you are constantly bombarding your mind with an influx of negative, suppressing images and information, how can you raise your vibration and good feelings towards yourself and the rest of humanity?

I threw my television out in 2008. I have barely watched any TV since, unless it's an interesting sports game, if I am staying in a hotel or happen to be at a friend's house when it is on. My children haven't watched television either and it's so noticeable when you talk to them. Their minds are free and active and not damaged in any way, shape or form through the negative cartoons and children's programmes that are shown on our TV screens. Don't get me wrong, there are some kids' programmes that are positive and teach and demonstrate great values, but the majority of the information is worthless and/or violent and depressing.

Why would you actually want to let your kids watch that?

The images that enter our minds are transmitted to our subconscious mind from our conscious brain and these images and thoughts held within the subconscious mind send signals to the Universe. This is how we create and control our lives. What we send out through our signals is the life we will create for ourselves. If the human race continues to soak up the depressing, war torn, poverty stricken image sent out to the world our energy will go where our focus goes and in turn more war and poverty will be created.

Wouldn't you rather have a happy life full of joy and peace? Of course you would. So why not fill your minds with pictures of joy, happiness and peace and let those thoughts, images and feelings filter through your internal system and flow right out into the world. This is how we can raise our vibration on a global scale as a global community, all living in harmony.

If you make the effort, others will follow you. The chain reaction will spread like wildfire, eating up and burning any negativity that's standing in its path. We have the power to change the world and raise its level of vibration, so we can end all wars, troubles and strife. It's time to bring back your power.

As you are changing your mindset right now, from reading this book, to one of peace and joy where your own world will be filled with a harmonious energy that emulates the ways in which you feel on a constant basis, why not let this joy spread throughout the world? Now that you are aware, make others also. Stand up and stand in your truth. Open your heart and open your mind and let the natural flow of the Universe take control, and fill your lives with happiness and bring a smile so pure to your face that it lasts through all eternity.

You have to bring back your power. From here on in make sure that you only feed your mind with information, images and thoughts that will aid you on your own personal journey. If you watch the news and watch the wars and starvation in certain parts of the world, you are only going to give your energy to it and so increase its energy in turn, and so give power to the troubles around the world. Start focusing your mind on the truth. The truth is that there is only peace and plenty of food to feed the world.

Control your life and let this fact be known to others that you can have a bountiful, pleasurable life. A maximum life in all areas if you take control right now. You are an inspiration to all who know you and also those that don't. Just by your new found energy you will radiate a glow of personal achievement and happiness and others will ask you, what do you do? Why are you so happy? You can let them know because you have discovered the truth. You know how to fulfil your life in the best possible way and that is by being happy. You can let them know that to be happy they just need to follow some basic principles, connect with the internal energy source of life itself, and choose their thoughts carefully, ensuring that any information that goes into their minds and is absorbed by the heart and soul is in perfect harmony and, as a result, love seeps through every pore in the entire body.

Another element to this process is to stop drinking alcohol. I have found since I stopped drinking that my connection to life has increased tenfold. I have become much more and my ability to communicate with the Universe and my angels and guardians has increased and my awareness has heightened. This has also increased my power. Why not also consider eating healthy organic foods with no chemicals? The chemicals in fast and packaged foods also harm and control our minds.

We should be putting love into our bodies, not poison. The more we respect our bodies the more our bodies will give us back. Let's start making small changes now and over time your entire lifestyle will have changed. I guarantee you, from personal experience with my family and many clients around the world, the fewer chemicals you put into your body, the happier you will become. You will have a sense of freedom come over you. It's hard to explain unless you have experienced it, but the chemicals in our foods enslave us, just like the television can manipulate our minds.

It's time to set yourself free.

Bring back your power!

Speaking To the Universe

*We shall not cease from exploration. And the end
of all our exploring will be to arrive where we
started and know the place for the first time.*

T.S. Eliot

People always ask me, 'How do you speak to your guides? How do
you communicate with the Universe, your Genie? How do you listen
and know they are speaking to you?'

Well these are very good questions. It took me a long time to know
and distinguish the difference between my ego and my inner voice,
or higher self, or God.

There are many different terminologies for what really is one and
the same. Your higher self or God is the messages that come directly
from the Universe itself. They are voices and/or messages that are
sent to guide you on your journey. Sometimes the Universe will speak
to you in signs. For example, you may see a sign on the road or hear a
fire engine. The Universe may be saying to you slow down, take care,
or perhaps making you be aware of how lucky and safe you are at
that particular moment.

When you live your life in a state of conscious awareness you can
ask questions and the answers will pop into your head. You will often
hear it like it's your own voice or the voice of another man or woman.
Normally the voices are soft and gentle. To hear them you must
trust and must be fully conscious, aware of your entire surroundings,
feeling totally alive and fully present.

Your ego on the other hand is not there to help you. Well actually it is. You know it's important that we discuss the ego carefully. If you decide to do something good your ego may be there saying no, don't do it. It's two fold. Firstly, it's challenging you to see if you can choose right over wrong and secondly it's there to make you aware that you need to get this voice of the ego under control. If you let your ego rule your mind you will end up travelling down paths of destruction and despair. You need to harness your ego and totally understand the difference between the two, your ego and your inner voice or higher self.

I found it difficult at first. As I came from a dark world and into the light later on so the ego played its part perfectly and used my weaknesses from my past to instil feelings from deep within that would make me think in a way in which I did not want to think.

I had to battle, from left to right, like a yoyo going back and forth. It was just like having the devil on one shoulder and an angel on the other, both telling me different stories. What should I believe? Who is right and who is wrong?

Firstly I quieten my mind and take deep breaths and allow my mind to empty. Once it does I let the soft spoken voice of my inner voice, the real me and not that of my ego, shine through and give me the necessary instructions to handle the situation correctly and constructively. The Universal Database has all the answers. Lying dormant in time and space is a seemless downloadable, infinite file of wisdom. We are all capable of tapping into it.

When you are thinking about taking action or something that has just happened to you, it's very easy to hear when the ego is trying to override you. More often than not it will shout at you, and so you know. There is a but, however. The ego can be cunning and manipulative and so will try and take on a different tone to trick you and you must be aware of this. If you are ever unsure do not make any rash decisions. Relax; if you don't do something today that you thought was urgent, don't worry. If you don't worry it will work out perfectly, it always does.

Again, quieten your mind, relax and forget about what you are trying to work out a solution for. Carry on with your life and the Universe will furnish you with your answer when you are ready to receive it. You will know instinctively, when the answer is coming from within. If you're unsure, wait, carry on and when you are 100% sure, go for it.

As well as your inner voice there are guides that we all have that are with us constantly. Go into a quiet space and relax. Breathe deeply and ask the universe to show you your guides. Tell the Universe that you are ready, open and willing to start receiving messages from your spirit guides and you would like to open the lines of communication. If at first it doesn't happen, don't worry.

Your mind must be relaxed and you cannot try and force the issue. If you get stressed because it's not happening then you need to be patient. More often than not you will not be ready and if you are aware and listening you will see messages from the Universe that will guide you to make you ready. There may be certain tasks that you have to accomplish or certain influences in your life that you may have to get rid of before they will allow you full access.

Quite often sugary foods stop the flow of communication between you and the Universe, you and your angels and guides. Know deep inside that this is what you want to do and let yourself go. Hand yourself over to the Universe, surrender yourself, and once you do the gates to heaven will open and the lines of communication will flow.

Remember this: the Universe wants to open your mind and channels between you and the magic out there. It doesn't want to hide it from you. It wants you to be an open channel but you must be open, willing and ready and when you can't communicate properly or it seems that it's not working just relax, as I said before. Meditate; empty your mind of any blockages and gunk that is stopping the universal flow.

There is only help and guidance from above, from around, inside and out. The spaces that fill up the Universe, in between objects and humans, are filled with a thinking substance, a creative energy that is always growing and thinking and trying to expand. It wants to increase your life and make it more harmonious so that you are living in bliss. Always remember this. It wants you to feel pure and happy. It wants you to feel an abundance of love because this magical force knows one thing, love for all. Love in all shapes and forms. Feel the love of the Universe, accept and cradle it and let it flourish and fill your entire being until you become a bouncing, bubbling, force of magical energy, working in perfect harmony with everyone and everything.

Start the process and empty your mind of any troubles and strife. Ask the Universe to take it away and use it for good wherever it's needed. Let the Universe use your past Achilles heel, take it away and turn it into light and positivity and be used for good wherever needed.

Once you open these lines of communication you will feel at ease with the world, knowing that you have the support of the most loving allies in the entire solar system. They will be there at your beck and call, ready to assist with anything and everything, and they will continue to love you regardless.

They will love with a love that you have never felt from any human being before because they love unconditionally and it's this unconditional love that we must pass on to the rest of the world.

Meet the Tree People

There is something greater and purer than what the mouth utters.
Silence illuminates our souls, whispers to our hearts, and brings
them together. Silence separates us from ourselves, makes us
sail the firmament of spirit, and brings us closer to heaven.

– Kahlil Gibran, *philosopher*

This earthly experience has so many hidden qualities. They are only hidden however to the untrained eye. Many children's fantasy films and books are based on so called mythical creatures; however, they are not mythical, they actually exist.

As kids we were open minded and could see so much. We came into this world with an open heart and an open mind – it's only the heaviness of this planet and the influences we have on us as we are growing up, that affect us and dampen down our senses. As little children we can see fairies, spirits and many other amazing spiritual beings.

A lot of the time our parents will say there's no one there, it was just a dream. These comments over time stop us believing and I was no different. I know lots of families now who encourage this ability to see and bring the best out in their children. Keeping them away from computer games and letting their minds be free to wonder and explore the true magic of life.

My wife and I let our children know what life is really like. From a young age, as long as they can remember, we have discussed fairies and angels and every night before bed we do positive affirmations. We encourage our children to go off in their minds and explore. At night time my kids don't want me to read them a story book – they want a story from my mind. We go into an imaginary library and pick a book and I make it up as I go along. All the time we are expanding our consciousness as we are not limiting ourselves to the parameters of the book, its pages and content. We go off and explore magical lands and my kids, more often than not, are the main characters in the story.

We have fairies, angels and many other spirit guides to help guide us and protect Mother Earth and the environment we live in. There are also other beings that have become a great part of my life. One of the reasons I was led to write this book was because of the fairies and also the tree people. The tree people you may ask, what are they?

Every living thing has a life force inside, a soul, a positive energy force that gives the object or living organism life. Inside every tree there is a soul that will talk to you in the English language or whatever language you would like to talk to it in. I love running out in nature and talking to the trees. Some people would say that I sound crazy. If you had told me about tree people ten years ago I would have thought you were crazy too.

When you release your mind and open the lines of communication you will see for yourself what really exists. I was out walking with my son one day and he felt tired and asked if we could sit down on a wooden bench right next to this old oak tree. I looked at the tree and saw what looked like a face in it, embedded within the bark on the trunk. I walked over and placed my hand on its trunk. 'Yes I am here,' said a voice. It was the life force from within the tree speaking to me. 'I am as real as you,' said a deep and kind voice, sounding ever so wise. I said to Josh, my son, to come on over but be careful not to stand on the roots. I don't know why I said it as I had climbed many a tree as a youngster but those words seemed appropriate at the time. After all I wouldn't stand on your feet if I came and spoke with you.

Josh placed his hand on the tree also and I asked him to tell me what he heard. 'The tree is talking to me, Dad,' he replied. I asked the tree how he was and he said, 'I am fine, how are you?'

'Isn't this cool,' I said to Josh, 'that we can communicate with the trees?' He was really happy. Trees themselves are very wise and again carry information millennia old. I encourage you to start communicating with all beings on this planet. Trees are also great healers. If you ever feel like taking a break from the hustle and bustle of the world go into nature and cuddle a tree. When you hug a tree like you would a loved one and tell the tree how much you love it that tree will respond with passion. I often find the oldest tree in the woods and hug it for what feels like an eternity. I get lost, I drift off into space and times disappears. The connection between you and the Universal intelligence you seek will open and flow like the Niagara Falls once you allow these wise beings of light to become a part of your natural human world.

You know we are at one with nature when we let our hearts fill up with love and we love ourselves unconditionally and also have a deep and profound sense of love and appreciation for every creation on this beautiful planet. We should love everything and everyone, including the trees, plants, animals, fish, birds and insects – regardless of what it is, it is living. Even the rocks and crystals have an inner consciousness. Everything in life is one. We are all made up of this same thing, energy. Energy in different shapes and forms but it all boils down to the same results. Everything in this entire Universe is made of a living, creating substance. A substance that thinks and that is alive.

We need to let go of the feeling that it's just us, here on this planet. Open your minds to endless possibilities and let the magic flow right back into your life. There are fairies and unicorns and all these wonderful creatures and they are not mythical – just like the tree people they are ready to inspire us, guide and nurture us as we move throughout our lives, growing spiritually, as we follow our path and continue on our journey.

Join force with these beings of light from another dimension. The very reason that we, as human beings, struggle to see them is because they are of a much lighter energy. Their vibration is much higher than ours. I've already mentioned that the energy here on Planet Earth is very dense, too dense for these magical beings to live amongst us every day, in a way in which we can see them. It would freak some people out if they saw a unicorn wandering down the street, but when the time is right they will appear in all their glory, letting humanity know that they are real and on our side, and here in this special place to help and protect us.

Ladies and gentlemen, beings of eternal light, please look deep inside and let your mind wander and explore the true magic that surrounds and lives between us. Rediscover your inner child and find that sense of fun and laughter. Fill your lives with it. Embrace it; don't be afraid of it. It's perfectly normal and if you can look back to the beginning of your life and unlock the memories stored inside your mind, in your in-house hard drive, you will remember what life was like and that back then you believed.

It's time to start believing again and rekindle that special relationship between you and the mythical kingdom of light. I am so, so happy for you. I am smiling from ear to ear right now as these messages are being relayed. Your journey is getting better and better. I love each and every one of you with all my heart and soul.

Love

I would rather have eyes that cannot see, ears that cannot hear,
lips that cannot speak, than a heart that cannot love.

– **Robert Tizon, author**

There is one extremely powerful force, and that is the force of love. It is love that keeps us grounded, love ensures we are safe, love cradles us and fills our hearts with joy and happiness. If someone is ill, unhappy or lacking in some way, shape or form in their lives, it's due to a lack of love.

It could be lack of love for themselves. It may be lack of love for their friends or lack of love for their job or family life. Some of us have hatred or jealousy towards others. There is no such thing as hatred or jealousy. It's just a lack of love and all we need to do, to fix any situation, is add more love to the mix.

We all want to be happy and flourish in all areas of our lives, so why not add love to the recipe of each and every situation and let your lives fill up with this incredible force. Love can conquer disease, negate jealousy and stamp out fear. Love really is the most powerful energy on this planet. We need to harness it and inject it into each and every part of our lives, health, love and money. We need to love everything and everyone and create a maximum life for ourselves.

Each and every beautiful human being on this planet deserves so much. Everybody deserves to live a maximum life and each and every human being, you included, as you read this right now, has the capability to go and achieve anything you want in this life. It all starts with love. You have to love yourself so much that you fill your entire mind, body and soul up with love. Then you can let the love overflow and spill into the lives of others.

You want happiness. You crave love. You desire peace. Why not make it happen? This book is opening your mind and my words are inspiring you from within. Let the love flow. If you tell another how much you love them and how important they are to you, it will make them feel very special. Why not start by letting everyone know how much they mean to your life, and mean it and feel it with all your power, when you tell them. Feel the love being projected from your heart to theirs and watch as the magic happens, right in front of your eyes.

We all want and thrive off love. We all want love and appreciation for our efforts, at home or in the world of business. Let gratitude flow in abundance from your heart to all who deserve to know when you interact with them. For those that you don't interact with, send them love through your heart and mind. This energy that fills the Universe is strong, and time and space are nothing to this force. You can be living in America and send love to London or Sydney – wherever you need to send it, send it.

If we all focused on what makes us truly happy then we can tip the world into peace, joy, love and harmony where there are no wars or famine. Wars and famine are an illusion anyway. Focus on peace and abundance and that's what the world will come into. All negativity will vanish forever as long we keep on minds fixed on the truth. The truth is that which makes us happy. Violence doesn't make us happy. Seeing people on the TV starving doesn't make us happy, so fix your attention on the truth, and pump your energy into it. Change the way in which you think and act, do it today for your sake and the current and future happiness of our children, and our children's children. Do it for them.

Let's unite, stand in our truth, love everything and everyone and focus our energies on that which we truly want.

Peace, love and harmony throughout the entire system. Now is the perfect moment. Over the last two years I have seen so many amazing human beings see the light and move towards it. Now it's your turn to stand up and be counted. Don't stand in the background, thinking everyone else will make it happen and enough human beings are working to bring peace, and it will all be fine.

We need to wake up the world at a rapid rate of knots. There is still a lack of love in many places, and in turn darkness. We need to move that dark to light and this will happen with the conscious effort of each and every one of us that knows the truth, If you didn't already, you do now, so use this knowledge wisely and go forth on your journey, as a spiritual warrior, blessing the Universe with your glorious presence.

Everything Needs Love

Just imagine that the purpose of life is your happiness only – then life becomes a cruel and senseless thing. You have to embrace the wisdom of humanity. Your intellect and your heart tell you that the meaning of life is to serve the force that sent you into the world. Then life becomes a joy.

– Leo Tolstoy

Each and every being, element or object in this entire Universe is meant to live in peace and harmony, in the company and surroundings of each other. Everything is a formation, derived from one energy source and this energy source makes up the entire system. The sun, moon, sky, trees, plants, animals and human beings, including every other possible object that you can see and also the parts of the universe that you cannot see.

There is a binding, loving connection that is instilled within all things, that makes up our Universe and when a part of this Universe suffers an attack, in the form of hatred, it becomes ill. More importantly, neglecting a part of our system, means that the part feeling neglected will suffer even more than if it is hated. What this solidifies in my mind is that we are meant to live together, we are meant to love each other unconditionally and we are aligned, perfectly, in such a unique fashion that without the attention and love from one another, our system falls apart.

Here is evidence to my claim. An experiment was performed. Two jars of cooked white rice were placed on two tables in two different rooms. One pot of rice was shown love and affection and the other jar was told obscenities, and how bad it was. The first jar stayed white and fresh but after a period of time the second jar was black and had started to decay.

Now, there was a third jar in the experiment, and this jar was left alone. My expectation was that this jar would be in a better state than the second jar, but it wasn't. It was blacker and more decayed than jar number two.

How is that possible?

What this means to me is that the rice, as a living substance, a part of the Universe, made up of the same formless substance that you and I are made out of, felt neglected, lonely and was given no attention and could not survive, without the energy of another being.

Now, similarly, a human being, who was awake spiritually, would have been in a better mental state having being neglected, than if he or she had been shown hatred and nastiness. The reason being, the human is at a stage of evolutionary growth where they understand the difference and can be happy, on their own, keeping themselves occupied.

Rice, on the other hand, even though it's made up of the same stuff you and I are made out of, is at a lower stage or form of life and has not progressed to a stage where it can think like you and me. It has, however, got feelings and that is why it decays through lack of attention.

If this happens with rice, it clearly shows that regardless of the stage of evolutionary growth a human being, object and any other life form is at, it has feelings and needs to be around other energy to survive. Now if all the energy being given out on Planet Earth was of a loving and caring nature, how amazing would life be and how happy would every human being, plant, animal and every other object on this planet be? Trees and plants would all be in a perfect state of health.

Mother Earth would be happy. If we fed her with love and affection she would return love and affection in abundance to each and every one of us. Love thy neighbour, love thy self. The same goes for Mother Earth and all of her inhabitants. Make sure that the next time you walk past a tree, building, plant or animal or any other part of this vast and amazing Universe that you smile and radiate positive energy.

Laughter and Playfulness

No matter how insignificant the thing you have to do, do it
as well as you can, give as much of your care and attention
as you would give to the thing you regard as most important.
For it will be those small things that you will be judged.

– Mahatma Gandhi

Living our lives with love is crucial to uplift the vibration here on
Earth and that of the vibration, throughout the entire solar system.
How we think, act and manage our lives has a profound effect on
every other planet in the entire galaxy.

To enhance the love in the world, we must bring laughter back into
our lives. We can bring laughter back into our lives by being children
once again. As we grow up so many of us start to believe that we must
emulate a certain way of being. We believe that we must conform, be
rigid and live life from a rule book.

What rule book are you reading and following? Is it the one where
you work to survive or is it a path that makes you happy, one where
you live to be happy and work because you choose that which you
enjoy? So many choose the former, and this is a life where we merely
exist and not live. It's a dull life where you miss out on so many
unique and wonderful experiences.

We need to bring back those days where we laughed uncontrollably
as children. You probably have moments now when you do but you
should be laughing until it hurts every day. Joy and happiness spring
from the seeds of laughter and playfulness. It's so easy to relegate
our minds to a dreary place in this dense environment, so focus

your energy on having fun. Whatever you decide to do with your life just make sure that you enjoy it, please, for the sake of all whose presences have graced this planet, past and present and for all those who again will return to bring peace and harmony and live in this earthly body again, at some point in the future.

Let's look at dolphins, incredible beings. They spend all day swimming, jumping and playing in the water, living their lives the way we should all live our lives. They are peaceful beings of light with so much love to give and a vibration so pure. The human race looks at dolphins as less primitive creatures but are they so? We look at angels as being a higher vibration and plants, animals, fish and vegetables as less so. Is this the way we should view our Universe?

If a potato were to speak to you it may say that I am here nestled in the ground having a big old party down here, vibrating at an extremely high frequency and the role I play sat here cuddled up in the ground is immense. My frequency keeps you humans balanced and affects the harmony in the world. If it wasn't for me the world may be different. The potato might go on to say and look at my friend over here in the field.

His name is Sycamore and he has a joyful and playful vibration and he lets all of his little helicopter sons and daughters fly out into the world to have fun on their own and plant themselves ready to grow into big sycamores themselves. And this is my friend apple tree. He is very sweet and the birds just love tasting the fruits he produces. They eat away and fly off when they are full and when they go to the toilet the seeds drop in different places so more apple trees can grow.

There are lots of us, the potato may go on to say, and we all have an extremely playful and harmonious vibration. We are all much more than the human race thinks we are. We all play our part in this magnificent play that you and everyone else is living in. It's like a big act and when you're acting you're supposed to be having fun. Why would you do a job if it wasn't fun, the potato may ask.

If it's not fun don't do it. This is just a game. A gigantic play with billions of characters. Enjoy your role because next time you audition for a part you may get to play me, the potato. You may not have any arms and legs and get to roam free across the land. You may be cuddled up here underground waiting to be picked and eaten. Be happy, love life and play your part with passion and pride.

Life must be fun. Life should be amazing. If it's not, a simple shift in your mind and emotions can change the course of your life and the course of many future lives forever. Play your part in this myriad of endings. Some are better than others and the choices we make right here, right now, on Mother Earth, will result in the forthcoming of the golden age, as long as we make the right choices.

There are a number of roads leading to an infinite number of destinations but the one that we all really want should be one of peace and harmony. No one likes the living order of hierarchy that has been developed by men and women's thoughts. Greed and glory has been in control for many years but the time is coming to an end.

Soon we will be turning on our TV channels to the delight of easy, vibrant news. News that fills us with hope, positivity and joy. No longer will we be forced to watch the opposing forces at work, infiltrating our minds with poisonous messages, turning our pure energies into those reckless types that get lost in a maze of ideas and emotions as we sit entranced by the media and the world news stations.

You already know how to bring back your power and now we are going one step further. You are not only bringing back your power but enhancing your ability to manifest a perfect life, a maximum life for you and the rest of humanity, by focusing on the good in you, one another and in all situations. Laughter and playfulness is the key. Bring it back into your life. Let it consume you with an ever-loving, corresponding moment of superiority as you venture into the present moment once again, knowing that you created this marvellous extravaganza.

It's your time to shine. Shine brightly with an ever increasing accuracy, with your sights set on the mark. The mark of love and peace. Together we shall shine brightly. Your brothers and sisters from heaven above are watching down as you and I and every other human being is finding the ecstasy, as they lift their internal life force, their spirit, as they understand the connection between the life force and the body and the bigger picture that affects us all as one universal community.

Be happy and laugh, be joyful and play. Have fun and create love, have warmth in your heart and flourish in the mystery of life.

Gratitude

Appreciation and gratitude are a must if you choose to become the architect of increased happiness and your own fulfillment.

– Doc Childre, founder of HeartMath

Gratitude is paramount to your success in creating a perfect life for yourself. Being grateful for every little thing that happens in your life will keep you in perfect harmony, with the Universe. Remember, the Universe is the supplier of your dreams and aspirations, and you must communicate with it at every opportunity.

The best way to communicate with the Universe or your Genie on a regular basis is through a deep and profound feeling of gratitude. If you thank the supply, the supply will give you more. Think about this for a second. If you do something for someone and they are not happy or kind with their words and don't thank you for what you did for them, will it make you want to do it again? If you help someone and they are grateful, thank you over and over and bake you a cake or give you a thank-you card to show how much your help meant to them, would you help them again? The answer to the first question is a firm big no and to the second one a great big fat yes.

If you thank the supply, the supply will give you more, and it always works. It's a universal law. If we take it, we lose it; if we create it, we keep it. If we give out negativity, we receive the same in return. If we give out positivity, we get back the same in equal proportion.

Think about your next-door neighbour or someone you know with a beautiful garden. Do you think they have a beautiful garden with flowers that bloom for a reason? They tend to their garden with love and they thank and bless their garden. You cannot have a garden that flourishes unless you tend to it with love and appreciation.

I know a man who grows oranges, a very successful man whose oranges are sought after by every person or company that uses oranges in their food or serves freshly squeezed orange juice. You will often find this man out in his orchards talking to the orange trees and whispering to them. If you saw him and didn't understand the law of attraction and the use of gratitude, you may think this man was crazy.

It's not luck that he has the best oranges in New Zealand. This man loves his work and loves the oranges he grows and loves the trees which produce the oranges. He constantly thanks the supply. Do you think it's any wonder that this man grows the tastiest, juiciest oranges around? Absolutely not!

Regardless of what the cards of life deal to you, gratitude must be first and foremost in your mind. Even if the circumstances seem to be the opposite of what you would have liked to happen, you must thank the person or the situation that the Genie has created.

Remember this. The universal mind, the Genie, knows more than you or I do. The Genie knows everything and often creates situations that on the outset look not too good, but once you have taken on board what has just happened, as long as you say thank you, you will always see that the reason it happened was for your greater good. Quite often in life, a seeming current failure could be the prelude to an almighty success.

Always be happy. Always be grateful even in the harshest of circumstances. I have come to realise that the Universe will test you, when you are on the brink of success, to see if you really have learned your lessons, and believe me, I have learnt mine. I am forever tested, but am forever grateful as I know in my heart that I am on the right track, and with absolute certainty, I go about my daily tasks and perform them well and thank everything and everyone in my life. As I do, I send them the feelings through my heart, not just saying thank you. You have to emit the feelings for the law of attraction to work and the Genie to come to your aid.

As you move forward in life and peel away the layers that will unlock the true greatness within, you may face challenges from opposing forces in the world. Acknowledge them, be grateful to them and smile, carry on and all will be OK. Gratitude is so powerful, it will aid you in ways I cannot explain. Just like love, gratitude is as special and will assist you in times of need. Remember this, however: do not lose touch with gratitude. Have an attitude to make gratitude a part of your daily existence.

Gratitude unlocks the fullness of life. It turns what we have into enough, and more. It turns denial into acceptance, chaos to order, confusion to clarity. It can turn a meal into a feast, a house into a home, a stranger into a friend. Gratitude makes sense of our past, brings peace for today, and creates a vision for tomorrow.

Drugs or Life?

There are no mistakes, no coincidences. All events
are blessings given to us to learn from.

– Elisabeth Kubler-Ross

We are coming to a point in this book where you will understand
all there is to understand about you and life itself. There is a place
within you that you are about to enter. Many people experience
something similar in life, and these experiences often come when
experimenting with drugs, particularly hallucinogenics such as
Ecstasy or Acid.

As a teenager and through other parts of my life, up until the point I
realised the truth, I have experimented with a wide range of drugs.
There have been occasions when I have experienced trips that have
taken me out of my body and made me feel very good indeed.

This high that is experienced whilst under the influence of drugs, can
be associated to that which you feel when you understand the truth
about life and the power that lies within. When you connect with the
power within you, the life force that is you, a sense of total perfection
overcomes you and the world itself looks very different from its usual
plain, grey and dismal view. Once you enter this special place, your
sense receptors heighten, just like they do on acid or ecstasy. Now,
having experienced both, the feelings felt by the natural state of
being, when in the present moment, as you stay still from the peace
within, are so much better.

Life itself in many other forms and states of being can also give
you the sense of the feelings you feel, when you are in the state of

awareness we are coming to in this book – the end result, that which we are all striving to discover, harness and remain in that place. Like painting a beautiful picture or sculpting the perfect work of art, or the rush you get when you ride the perfect wave or the feeling of fulfilment at the time of orgasm, during sexual intercourse. All of these feelings, mixed together at the critical point of fulfilment and total satisfaction, are what you can feel every moment of your life.

You can live your life in this state of being, once you are woken up, fully aware and you do not need drugs to take you to this place. In fact, drugs will only obstruct your passageway to this perfect place of Zen.

Imagine living your life every day, excited like a little child, waiting for Father Christmas to come down the chimney, with a bag of presents. How would you like that moment of sexual excitement, at the point of climax, to be how you feel every second of every day? That rush you feel when you are freefalling from a plane on your first skydive can be how you live your life each and every moment, once you are in tune with the natural song, played by the Universe.

It took me years to find this place. I am giving you a quick route to the end result and as you read on the process will accelerate and you will find yourself in this special place, being totally aware.

Looking back now I believe that is what I was chasing, when I spent my years taking drugs. I was searching for paradise. A place where I could feel alive, happy and at peace, with no care in the world. I came close on many occasions but as with all temporary fixes, they fade away and you feel worse than you did before you started.

Once you connect with source and discover the inner you it will be much the same. You will have periods where you are at peace, sitting in the stillness that protects you and other times you will slip back out. This is normal and you should never worry. The more you go to this place or invite this state of being into your daily life, the more it will hang around until it eventually consumes you and your life becomes a constant scene or magical moment from a fairytale.

Travelling

I am not on this earth by chance. I am here for a purpose and that purpose is to grow into a mountain, not to shrink to a grain of sand.

– Og Mandino

About one year into my past life regressions with Trish at The Tree Of Life Centre, she gave me a book to read, a fictional book but one that resembles the truth in all things. The book is called The Traveler and it has a sequel called The Dark River.

The books are about travellers who are able to bring their light, their spirit, from their bodies and walk through time and space. The travellers in the story are two brothers and they are protected by a set of people – I would call them real life guardian angels. They protected the travellers from the Brethren, a group of people that ran the world through systems and control. They wanted the travellers dead as they could elude the system and were uncontrollable.

The system was referred to as the grid and total control was the aim of the leaders of the Brethren. They spent their lives chasing down, searching for and trying to destroy the travellers. Maybe this resembles our government in the world we live in today?

These books were written by a man by the name of John Twelve Hawks. I would like to commend you, John Twelve Hawks, for writing and publishing these books. From the bottom of my heart to yours, I salute you, brother.

Whether Trish gave me this book consciously or subconsciously, I am not sure. Obviously she knew she was giving it to me but was she expecting the desired effect it would have upon me? Knowing Trish, I believe so and am grateful she furnished me with her copy. I flew through it in two days.

The first thing I did after completing the book was to get on the phone and ask when I could go travelling. 'On your next session' was the reply. I was so, so excited, like a little kid waiting for Santa Claus, to make the appearance on Christmas Eve.

I went to the barn as usual, made myself my regular mug of camomile tea and waited for Trish to finish her appointment. What I love about Trish is that she will see you for as long as necessary. Quite often I would wait or others would wait for me to finish. But everyone had an understanding; each soul was patient as they understood the work and the great benefits to all. They were also aware of leaving Trish's room, with work still incomplete, was not the best situation for the mind, body and soul, so a common reality of understanding and respecting each other's needs was met. Perfection.

It was eventually my turn and in I went. I sat down in Trish's chair but this time the formality was different. There was no golden bubble, smile, field or tree of life. I was asked to simply sit in my chair and breathe deep and slow. I was asked to relax my mind and just focus. Trish spoke to me and soothed my mind, putting it in the perfect state for what was about to happen.

I breathed deeper and longer, even deeper and slower than ever until it felt like my heart was beating once a minute, it was so surreal. I focused on bringing myself out from my body and eventually the strangest thing happened. It was like I, me, Jerry Sargeant, had risen out of my body. It was not me, however, it was my soul, my light. It still felt like me, though. I turned around and was looking back at myself slumped in the chair as though I was asleep. At the same time, though, I was looking through my eyes and could see Trish sat opposite me. It was like I was in two places at once. I felt so light and free. Who was in the chair and who was walking or floating around? There was total separation. I was two forms, in two different dimensions.

It was clear to me that Jerry Sargeant was in the chair but the energy, my soul or spirit, the real essence of who I was, had lifted or risen out from inside the body and broken free.

This experience happened shortly after the incident in Romania where I saw the lifeless vessel lying on the ground. These two experiences in quick succession were instrumental in my journey. They gave me great understanding.

I walked through the wall behind Trish and out into the barn. 'I can see a man in a checked shirt,' I said and Trish replied, 'Yes, he's often here, he's harmless. He comes to visit from time to time.'

I then walked through the next wall and out into the driveway that leads from the road to the barn, where Trish does her work. I am going to go to my house, I remember saying to Trish and before you knew it, as soon as I had thought it I was there, stood outside my house. I walked inside and into the kitchen and watched Laura making dinner for the kids. I even watched her ship Josh into line as he was annoying his big sister. How amazing is this? I thought. This is so cool.

I stayed for a few moments and then went straight back to the barn. I stopped outside and then walked through the wall again and back inside. Later that evening I asked Laura if when she was making the kids dinner she had had to have a word with Josh and she confirmed it to be true. Even though I trusted I had to ask the questions. It was the first time I had done this, after all.

After arriving back in the barn I saw two beautiful little girls in white dresses – they looked like twins. They walked up to me. I asked Trish if she could see them too and she replied 'yes'. They looked at me and smiled and when they did their teeth were all pointy and sharp as razors. They looked like two beautiful devils in disguise.

I asked them what they wanted and they replied, 'you', looking at me with their evil grins. They wouldn't say anything else and Trish told me to come back in the room. I walked back through the wall and stopped for a moment to look at myself, still slumped in the chair. It was amazing, strange, weird and crazy all at once. Looking at myself I looked lifeless, helpless and useless, without any life force inside. A totally different sight to that which you see in the mirror.

I turned around and sat back down into my body and within a split second I was there, back in the room and it all seemed normal again. It drained my energy and I had to sit there for a while and come back around. It was like I was dazed but high as a kite at the same time. What an experience.

Trish asked if I was OK and I replied 'yes' with a big cheesy grin on my face. I questioned her about the two little girls and what that experience was about. Trish said, 'Let's leave it until next time. We will deal with it then.'

I left the barn that evening feeling like I had just lifted the World Cup and the whole country was cheering for me. I felt exhilarated, like I had achieved something spectacular. Well I had, I had just travelled. Trish said to me don't be disappointed if you can't do this first time around, but not once did I doubt my abilities. I knew it would be a success.

I knew the human body and the soul relationship was unique and this was the first time I had seen and felt the connection and the separation, both at the same time, in all its glory. I was so proud of myself and so happy.

Two Beautiful Girls and A Lonely Soul

How can you hesitate? Risk! Risk anything! Care no more
for opinions of others, for those voices. Do the hardest thing
on earth for you. Act for yourself. Face the truth.

– **Katherine Mansfield**

When I arrived at home I couldn't stop thinking about these two
girls. They were beautiful yet when they smiled there was malice
in their soul. What could it mean? How could I find out more and
release these girls from their seeming torment?

I was shattered when I got home and took a shower and then went
and had some food with Laura and told her all about this experience.
I then went upstairs and into Aalayah's bedroom to give her a kiss
and cuddle and read her a story. As I was leaving her room I saw
these two same girls, dressed in white, exactly as I had seen them in
Trish's barn and they were looking at me. A heaviness set over me
and I felt quite strange. I tried to communicate with them and all
they would say is that they wanted to punish me for what I had done.

What had I done? How could I reverse the problem? What could
I have possibly done to hurt or affect these two beautiful girls in a
negative way? They were clearly stuck in the in-between world. Some
human beings that die, their souls cannot pass from the realm the
human body dies in, here on Earth and back to the ball of light, spirit
or heaven. They get stuck as they may have some unfinished business
or something they can't let go of.

After this particular incident I started doing clearing work and
helping souls pass through. You wouldn't believe how many get stuck.

Untold amounts.

Twenty four hours later, the feelings in me of darkness and misery were growing and I kept seeing these girls everywhere, as though they were there in the room with me. I phoned Trish and managed to get an emergency appointment, at about 10 that evening. Trish has thousands of clients and is booked up months and months in advance, but this was getting serious and she agreed to help me solve this issue as soon as possible.

I sat down in the chair and we had a long discussion with the girls. It was something that had a huge effect on my life. Four years earlier I had a business and we built property portfolios for our clients. It was a great business up until the point the property market crashed in 2004. We could not fulfil on our obligations to our clients, on the contracts we had signed with them, and we went bust. We lost everything – and more importantly so did the clients.

There were lovely human beings that had invested their life savings into our company and they lost it all. One particular gentleman was broken and could not face his family and so ran away and left them. He had a wife and two daughters.

All of this became clear as the girls were unveiling their hatred towards me and their passion to see me suffer. I was not aware of this up until this point in time. They continued to tell the story, and how, after their father had left, their mother had gassed herself and the girls in her car.

The mother had passed on through but the girls were stuck. They told me that I had grown spiritually and had learned from my mistakes and that they were happy to sacrifice themselves for the greater good of the Universe. They said I had something to present to the world and that my services are much needed and that they knew when they came down into this earthly experience, that this would be the outcome.

They were tormenting me to get my attention and they saw the opportunity when I went travelling to act and seize the opportunity to communicate properly. They said that they are stuck, however, and they would like to reunite with their mother. We all work in soul groups and their mother was waiting for them on the other side.

Even though she would still be spirit on the other side, back in heaven, she wanted to know that they had made it back through.

Trish and I put on a suit of light each, to protect ourselves as we walked through the in-between world to reunite these two lovely angels with their mother. It's a place like nothing I have experienced or can ever really properly describe. It exists and is not the nicest of places. Somewhere I would not like to reside.

After some mental preparation we walked into this room. It was more like a huge cave or cavern, an area of blackness and torment, and there were so many souls all over us, trying to drag us down or suck us in to whatever they were trying to suck us into.

I was told to focus on the door at the end and keep my mind on the job at hand. It took us several minutes to trudge our way through and reach the door. When we opened it there was the mother, sat on a bench, waiting for her daughters. We reunited them and thanked them for this experience. They just drifted off and vanished into light. When we opened the door to see the mother sat on a bench, I looked around and this place was so beautiful. It really is heaven there. It is filled with a white, almost silver-white light. A light so pure and clean and the energy there is like nothing I have ever experienced. It's certainly not a place to fear, but more a shrine of peace, to embrace when your time comes to move on.

As we turned to walk back through, thousands of spirits, like an army of bats flying up through a cave, bolted towards the door. They poured through and I couldn't shut the door. It took both Trish and I, and all our mental strength and power to get that door shut. Once we did we refocused and came back through the corridor we had walked through and back through the heart and the smile and back into the room.

Just another day at The Tree Of Life Centre but the unveiling of another set of useful skills that I had acquired. It's actually a set of skills that we are all capable of acquiring if we open our minds and our hearts to the magnitude of this beloved Universe and all its airs and graces.

This experience taught me so much and I felt privileged to be a part of the grand master plan. You too are a part of this plan. You too have the courage and power, the faith and love to make a difference here in your life. Harness your greatness and channel it constructively and make the most of every moment, here on Planet Earth. Let's spread the message and ride the wave into eternal glory so we can reap the benefits, in this lifetime, and many more to come.

Love and Light.

Whenever I'm Away

I know of no more encouraging fact than the ability of a man to elevate his life by conscious endeavour. It is something to paint a picture, or to carve a statue, and so make a few objects beautiful. It is far more glorious to carve and paint the very atmosphere and medium through which we look. This morally we can do.

– Henry David Thoreau

What I am going to share with you now is how your past lives can affect the way in which you think in your present lifetime and demonstrate that past and present are intertwined, not forgetting the future of course. What we must remember, however, is that the only moment you can ever truly harness is the present moment. When we arrive in the future, it's still the present moment. When we travel to a past life, we are still there in the present moment, at the time we arrive.

This was one of the first few past lives I ventured into, as I had a pressing issue that needed some attention. I used to have not such good feelings when I phoned Laura and I couldn't get in touch with her. If I called and she didn't answer, I would call her maybe fifteen to twenty times and if she still didn't pick up the phone, I would have the most horrific thoughts going through my head. I used to think that someone had gone into my home and taken my family or murdered them there and then on the spot.

These are not the sort of things one likes to think each and every time your loved ones don't answer the telephone. It drove me crazy, but I could not stop it. I was still exploring past life regression at this stage and wasn't sure how or if it could help in anyway; however, I mentioned my misuse of the mind and the lack of control I had over these messed-up images, that were running right through me and taking control of my soul.

Trish asked me to sit down in the chair as usual and in we went. When we asked to be taken to a level I ventured down this long corridor and eventually ended up many years ago in the Saxon times. I was a middle aged Saxon warrior and the men of our tribe were on a big old wooden boat, packing up all our belongings. The women and children were back on what I would refer to as a reservation, even though that is what I believe the correct terminology is used for the Native American Indians. A camp seemed too modern so for me I can only describe it as a reservation.

As we were loading up the boats and getting ready to set sail, working hard and going as fast as we could, I sensed a matter of urgency as we were working but wasn't sure why. The next thing another tribe of warriors on horseback came over the hill and down into our reservation, where the women and children were.

What happened next had obviously scarred me for hundreds of years, through how many lifetimes, I can't be sure. The warriors slaughtered most of the women and children before us fellow warriors had a chance to rush back and save them. My wife had her throat slit and my children were trampled on by horses. They were the same souls as that of my wife and children in this life I am living today.

I saw it all as clear as day, as I was running back from the boat to save them; however, it was inevitable. I was too late and I lost the most precious parts of my life. I spoke to the past aspect of my soul and let him know that I was the future progression and that I was with Laura, Aalayah and Josh in this lifetime and that I was protecting them and they were very happy. Even though they would not have been called by those names back then, that's how I spoke to him. He was grateful that I had come to see him and I gave him a huge, almighty cuddle and brought him home. He turned to light and positivity and back through the heart I came until I was sat back in the room with Trish.

Ever since that day I have had no more feelings when Laura doesn't answer the phone. If she doesn't I have a real sense of calm come over me as if to say it's OK now, nothing to fear. Your family are safe, they are being guided. They always will be and so will you. You are all divine beings of light and the Universe will be there, to ensure your safety at all times.

You see when we come into our lives, our human bodily format, we have lessons to learn. If we don't learn them, it's inevitable we will come back again and have the opportunity to learn, a second, third or maybe fourth time around. We will keep coming back until we get it. Understand it and learn the lesson as that is the order of the day. The much needed lessons for our own personal spiritual growth.

Many souls commit crimes. I don't even like mentioning this as the aim is to focus on the light and the good and what it is that we want; however, we have a message to relay, so will do so for the sake of the greater good. Murder is something that one should find hard to break the pattern of. I have committed this hideous crime in many of my past lives and the last five all in a row. This life I am living today has been a huge turning point for my soul and its growth. I started out in life and have been down a road very similar to many other past lives but this time around I have managed to turn the tide. I managed to break free from the chains that have shackled me for hundreds of years. Now I can grow. I have entered the light in all its glory.

I have accomplished something I am very proud of, both on a physical and spiritual level as my past life regressions at The Tree

Of life have shown me what a mountain of a challenge I faced in this body, as Jerry Sargeant. The rewards of changing the course of time are immense. I now have the opportunity to share with the world, my experiences and lead by example. I have set the record straight and have now altered the course of my future experiences. Will I come back down again to Planet Earth? Maybe I will, maybe I won't.

Who knows?

What I do know is that from here on in I have grown in many ways and can be a shining example to many of my soul mates, on their own personal journeys. We all need inspiration and motivation to lead us into the light. When you see yours, take it. Maybe this book was the last piece of your own puzzle, and now you too can step into this world of peace and happiness, that I now choose to live in.

So many human beings themselves are shackled by their daily experiences, work, money, health, love or lack of it should I say. Whatever your personal circumstances are, you can change them. You can change anything by making a conscious decision to change. Once you make that conscious decision, back it up with affirmative action and set your new precedence here on this rich and bountiful planet.

It's there in front of you, ready for the creating. Start the creation process and jump on the train that will take you forward, to a happy place in your heart. One where you only know joy and laughter because it's time to excel in the kingdom you are creating. My love is with you always.

Oh My Gosh

With life I am on the attack, restlessly ferreting out
each pleasure, foraging for answers, wringing from
it even the pain. I ransack life, hunt it down.

– Marita Golden

This was hard for me to accept, until I shred myself of my ego. I had lived with this dream for many years, up until the point, and now I had someone to ask questions regarding it, a special human being in my life to help me understand the connection and why this was happening.

As a child and a teenager I used to have this reoccurring dream that made no sense, but at the same time didn't feel odd, when really it should have felt very odd. Maybe disgusting in fact. Well to the unaware human being, this would have been off the chart and some people may have wanted me to have psychiatric help.

When I was born I was fostered and eventually adopted. Now every relationship we have here on Earth is linked, it's connected to other lives in the past, present and future. We cannot change this. All we can do is change the outcome to one that is good, by making the right choices in this life right now.

If you can imagine this. I have a wife and two children, a son and a daughter. Souls work in soul groups and we connect lifetime after lifetime teaching each other lessons. Sometimes we may skip a lifetime or two, apart from each other, but in the grand scheme of things a lifetime or two is like a drop of rain in the vast ocean.

My wife could have been my daughter of my father before. My daughter now, has certainly been my mother several times over and maybe my father also. We connect and re-connect and not always as the same gender. Some people find this hard to swallow but it's the reality of this enormous Universe we live and play in.

Back to my dream.

I used to have this dream that I was having sexual intercourse with this beautiful young lady, our bodies would be rubbing and the passion was extremely intense. Each and every time I had this dream it would be exactly the same. What happens next is the freaky part. This beautiful, gentle, angel of a woman with long brown hair and gorgeous brown eyes turned into my mother. Imagine that. You are having the best sex ever and then all of sudden you are doing it with your mum. At that point I would wake up in a ball of sweat, every time.

Why would this be happening was the question I asked Trish one day. It took me eighteen months before I mentioned this to her. It was easy to tell her when I did but I just kept this one locked away in a dark, deep chamber in my mind, for many years. I had thrown away the key and it was to rot in the depths of my mind. Telling Trish, who by this time had become a dear friend to me, was the best thing I ever did.

So off we went into my subconscious store house of riches where all the answers lie, untouched and in perfect condition, waiting for the great unveiling, to assist us on this current path. We were taken back to just before the Spanish wars. There I was with the beautiful lady from my dream. She was my wife and she was pregnant with our first child.

I had to go off to fight and was gone for a very long time. My wife did not like the fact that I had gone off to battle and left her with our unborn child and so she decided to use an ancient method of abortion and get rid of the unborn baby. She did it after three months of being pregnant however. It's at three months that the soul comes into the body and resides there, ready to start forming the bond and also forgetting any past life experiences. We have to forget them or the lessons would be too easy to learn.

I actually stayed in Spain after the wars and never came home. My wife never forgave me. We had much more to learn together on a soul level.

Now, my adoptive parents tried to have children of their own but could not. My mother was not allowed to give birth in this lifetime as a punishment, or more so a lesson learned, for aborting the last child all those years ago. So she decided to adopt and who did she get? Yes me, her former husband and now her adopted son.

It's no wonder that our relationship has been so turbulent, during all the years I was growing up. I didn't really understand my mother until I was thirty one years of age, and we sat and discussed my childhood and how we both felt. It was like a huge burden had been lifted off both of our shoulders. Understanding my mother for the very first time was a fulfilling experience, and one I will cherish forever.

We are all connected at source in many ways, not just one. Accept this and you will unlock memories from deep inside you that will enable you to come to understand why, what and how events, people and circumstances happen. Once you unlock this potential you will carve a new paradigm, you will etch it into your make-up and have a different way of looking at and exploring current issues or challenges. It's so liberating to be finally free and to understand on a deep level the enormous intermingling of lives.

Start exploring, I commend you.

Follow Your Instincts

The World is a great book, of which they who
never stir from home read only a page.

– St Augustine

Let me take you back to when I was seventeen years of age, in this current lifetime. I want to show you how the Universe can guide you and send walk-ins into your life to bring you back on track. Walk-ins could be angels or unconscious agents of the Universe, helping you stay on track. They can walk into your life, out of nowhere, like a knight in shining armour, coming to save the day.

Between fourteen and sixteen, coming on seventeen years of age I was on a downwards spiral of self-destruction. I had turned to drink and drugs, moved out of home and was travelling the UK countryside indulging in the rave scene at the time. Loud music, ecstasy and whistle-blowing was my life.

I knew I had to change my ways as I was on a collision course for either an early grave or a bed within HMP (Her Majesty's Prison). So I decided to get a job and save as much money as I could, so I could get out of England with my girlfriend, away from any influences and straighten myself out.

I got a job working in a factory, taking on board all the hours I could get and within a year had saved enough money. Our plan was to buy an old van and go off travelling around Europe. We had a date set and we were off. The night before we left we were in the pub saying our farewells and having a drink.

This man, whom we had never seen or met before, walked in and walked up to us. He said he had heard we were going travelling and that we should take this piece of paper. On it was a name and number. He said, 'Don't go travelling – go to Tenerife instead.' He said, 'Phone this guy and he will give you a place to stay and you will earn at least three hundred pounds a week.'

We didn't even question him. We sold the van the next day and bought two one-way tickets. I didn't know back then that I was being guided. It just felt right, the sun and money and free accommodation probably helped, but off we went nonetheless.

If I hadn't made that decision and gone to Tenerife, my whole life would have been different. I actually went to a place where the influences around me were ten times worse, and I was involved in many things I am not proud of in the years I spent there.

It was here that I made some contacts including the one that eventually led me to The Tree Of Life Centre. I also met my rock whilst in Spain – my beautiful wife Laura – and our first child was born there. I also learnt how to sell, a trade that has aided me throughout my life.

Many things good and not so good happened in Tenerife. The good elements were blessings and the not so good elements were huge tests for me, to try and imbed me in the darkness forever. I won't lie to you. It almost did. For many years I was locked into a shadowy world of ill being.

It was my wife that re-entered my path, in this lifetime, to start the process of liberating me from my shackles. She taught me what love really was. I thought I had loved up until this point but not like this. Laura is a strong woman and has much love to share and this strong, loving character, setting the record straight for me, was the best gift

I have ever received. It came at the perfect moment. Just like all who are lucky enough to be aware and take on board the guidance of others. There have been times in this life with Laura that I could have easily strayed back off track, but knowing she was there and the thought of losing her kept me in check.

Behind every good man there is strong woman and behind every good woman there is a strong man. Laura, I love you dearly, with all my heart, always and forever.

So when you get a gut instinct, listen and follow it. It will be your Genie telling you that you're off track and that this is the way forward. Listen and read the signs. Follow your heart and always be aware that there is a greater force in this world that knows much more than you or I.

Old Communication

The ultimate measure of a man is not where he stands in moments of confidence but where he stands at times of challenge and controversy.

– Martin Luther King Jr

Seventy eight thousand years ago there was a country or a place called Atlantis. Many think this world was just a myth and maybe another fairytale or story. I am telling you right now that world did exist and it will, once again, rise up when the time is right and the order has been set.

I have been back to Atlantis and seen exactly what it was like. It was like going back to the future. Atlanteans were a very advanced race. They had cars that flew through the air and communicated with the use of their minds. Telepathy was the way they communicated. They were so advanced, too advanced maybe for that time and space.

What happened back in Atlantis was perfect in the great order but could have, on the other hand, been avoided. The Atlanteans used their minds to control people and enslave them mentally and as a result physically. The Universe was tipping out of balance and something had to be done.

Much like this planet we are living on here and now, in this time and space. There are darker forces at work and they have tried to use control in different shapes and forms, to stop us from believing in ourselves, by dampening our spirits through the use of technology. Computer systems, television, radio, they are all used to influence the minds of us human beings, here on Planet Earth.

They fill our minds with information that will not benefit us in any way, shape or form. They poison our minds with war and crime and make the foods that most of humanity can afford unhealthy, full of chemicals and garbage, that again can only dampen our spirits.

If we all understood what I now know, we can rise above and out of this state, where a lack of light has embodied us. We are not far off finding that tipping point. That tipping point, where more than fifty percent of the world becomes aware, is not far off. If we pull together now we can raise global consciousness and make a real difference to the future of our world.

When we understand and become aware we can open the lines of old communication, where we can speak with the use of our minds. No more telephones. Eventually we will have no need for transport because we will be able to teleport ourselves from one place to another. Again this is not that far in coming. The quicker we can raise the vibration here on Mother Earth the faster all of these exciting circumstances will unfold.

Do you know that we only use five percent of the human brain? Imagine what will happen when you unlock the true potential of the most powerful tool that you possess. Stop letting the not so good news infiltrate and control your mind. Remember your thoughts and both your subconscious and conscious mind work in unison to bring you the life you want. Ensure the thoughts you let bypass the security system have authority to enter and deserve a place of rest in your life-developing instrument. Really, ladies and gentleman, I cannot stress enough how important this matter is.

Soon Atlantis will rise again and it will be a glorious moment. When we get to this stage we will all be communicating the way we should be, some of us probably before. Some of us already do – those that are aware and practise this method. The more you practise the easier and more naturally it will flow.

When you do regain this amazing gift you must put it to good use.
Don't for a second think you have the right to coerce another human
being with mental forces just because you have the power to do so.
That power is liberating; however it will be stripped away from you
just as quickly as you attained it.

Use your mind, right now, to shine light. Shine an abundance of
light all over the world and let it be known that you are waking up
and regaining your magical powers. You are rediscovering your true
potential as you and I and every other spiritual warrior on this planet
are stepping forward. We are standing up and being counted at the
critical tipping point where the human race, as a whole, will become
equal, and be reborn under a new time and age. One of peace and
harmony.

My heart goes out to you with blessings from above.

Checkmate

Do not wait for life. Do not long for it. Be aware, always at every moment, that the miracle is in the here and now.

– E. E. Cummings

As I am writing this chapter I am sat in the Roosevelt Hotel in Los Angeles. I am here for a book signing and yesterday I met a really interesting gentleman, whom I know will become a very good friend.

I was telling him a story about an incident that happened to me on the plane I took, from New Jersey to LA, on my way here. He said, 'That would make a great chapter right there, Jerry.' So I dedicate this chapter to my new friend Alain Renailt, from Canada.

Two days ago I boarded a plane from New Jersey to Los Angeles and I ended up speaking to this lovely lady on the plane and gave her a copy of my book. This incident tells the story of how the Universe has fine-tuned and manoeuvred people and events to make two people connect. It will show you how the ego and negative influences in our mind can try and stop you from achieving your greatest good.

I love incidents like this as they show the Universe, in all its glory, hard at work, to ensure that each human being is in the right place, at the right time.

So I get on the plane and walk to find my seat. When I get there a lady is sitting in it. So I explain that that's my seat. She looks flustered and says, 'No this is my seat, are you not sitting there?' Her husband, who is sat next to her but across the aisle says, 'There's plenty of seats back there.' So I see that they really want to sit there, they looked a little stressed, and so I proceeded to the back of the plane, and sat down in an empty seat.

I sat down and there was about twenty minutes before we were due to take off. Now I knew that more people may be coming on. What happened next was so perfect to watch and be a part of. The plane started filling up and a man came and said to me that I was sitting in his seat, so I moved. Then a lady came and approached me and said, 'You're sitting in my seat, sir.' So again I moved. This happened several times until there was nowhere left to sit.

Well, there was nowhere left to sit apart from the one place on the entire plane, my original seat. So I go back to the lady that was first sitting in my seat and say, 'I am sorry but I have tried my best but there is nowhere else to sit.' Checkmate. The Universe brought me back to this seat because I had to connect with this lady. So she moves one seat to the right and the guy that was sitting in her seat picked up his bag and went somewhere else. I am not sure where because there was nowhere else to sit. It was like he just vanished.

The lady apologises to me and thanks me for trying to help her out. I was being kind, but I also knew, as I watched the live, real time game of chess being played, with me and this other lady as two human kings, I knew that eventually I would be back where I was supposed to be, sitting in my seat, so the Universe could connect the two of us. I didn't know why. I just knew it would happen.

Now what's bizarre – no not really bizarre but fascinating – is that when I start talking to this lady she asks me what I am doing in Los Angeles. I tell her I am an author and travelling to a book signing. We engage in conversation and she starts to open up about her life. She has been through some recent experiences and is in need of some direction and motivation. I tell her about my book The Magnet and The Genie 'Maximum Wealth' and how it's about creating a maximum life in all areas, health, love and money and how there is a set of principles, a method to follow and if she were to follow it, her life would change in a positive way. So she asks where she can buy a copy.

'I can do better than that,' I said and pulled a copy from my bag, signed it and gave it to her. She was very happy. 'This is just what I needed,' she said. 'I think we were supposed to sit next to each other,' she added. I looked at her and smiled.

Now what she proceeded to tell me next is the most amazing part of this story. When I first approached this lady to inform her she was in my seat, she looked flustered. This is the reason why. Both she and her husband were due to fly from Chicago to LA. Something happened at Chicago, they could not take their plane as it was grounded, and so the airline arranged a car to take them to Newark airport so they could get a connecting flight to LA. It was all a crazy rush and they only just made it so no wonder she was feeling rushed and not grounded, certainly not her normal self.

What else is amazing about this story is that when I booked my flight to travel from the UK to LA, I spoke with the travel agent and was told it was a direct flight. When I received my tickets on the e-mail, there was a stop in New Jersey, at Newark airport. There was a split moment when I briefly thought, oh great, an extra three hours on my journey. It only lasted for about five seconds however as I quickly backed up and re-directed my thoughts to that of gratitude, and that there must be a reason why this has happened.

As you see, there was – it was total perfection. I had to sacrifice a few hours of my time for the greater good, to assist this wonderful human being in her time of need. I am so happy that I did and I didn't let my ego push me into phoning back the travel agent and demand she reissue the correct tickets.

Taking this flight also meant I lost a day in LA on the way back but what is cool and more important is the fact that I got to see my family a day earlier. So always look for the good in all situations, regardless of your reaction; there will always be a reason why and it will always be for the good of the human race.

There was a window of opportunity that she had to connect with me and for me to give her this book. How amazing is it that a mind that knows more than both you and I and the rest of the human race, conjured a plan and executed it with precision and accuracy, down to the point where we sat next to each other.

Now the lady was in a flustered state, so her ego, the not so light side of the force as such, the part that tries to control in a negative capacity and influence us human beings who are not aware, tried its best, to ensure I sat away from her. It even influenced the mind of her husband also, as he asked me to move to the back also, where there were plenty of seats.

The ego didn't want my help. It didn't want the lady to connect with me. It wanted her to suffer and remain in darkness with a candle on its last legs about to go out and leave her feeling alone and afraid. The light side, the good side, the force of nature that knows what's best for each and every soul on this planet, had stopped a plane in Chicago, arranged for a car to be available to get this beautiful couple to the airport in New Jersey, so that they could board the plane, and be on the same flight as me.

Now the lady could have sat where the husband was sitting but she sat where she sat and where I was supposed to be sitting. The Universe had every last tiny detail of this master plan arranged with absolute perfection.

Do you really think that the Universal mind of absolute perfection was going to let the negativity in her mind from being flustered and rushed, stop me from sitting next to her after it went to all this trouble? No way. Not in a million years.

If you let life unfold naturally and go with the flow, ride the wave and follow your dreams you will find peace and happiness. Each and every situation is a miracle if you look at it with eyes that are open, not through a misty fog that hinders the true and breathtaking reality we are living in.

This lady went through worry and stress, thinking she would miss her plane, get stuck in the snow in Chicago or maybe in traffic, and miss the Newark flight. If she was aware she could have sat back, relaxed and thanked the Universe for what was happening. Even if she didn't know why. It all became clear though. She said herself, 'I think I was supposed to sit next to you.'

She knew it herself once the jigsaw puzzle had been pieced together. Never underestimate the one that knows everything, the Genie, the Universe, before it has a chance to complete the puzzle. It will unfold and each piece will be placed immaculately, where it is supposed to be and the result will be perfect, always.

You have to trust. Trust is so important. You are in a totally different place right now from when you started reading this book. I am so happy that your consciousness is growing and expanding, you're thinking differently. In a way in which your life will get better and better. You are allowing more and more magic into your life and I can feel the happiness radiating throughout your entire being.

You are so special. I am looking down on you now with a huge smile on my face. You are beautiful, intelligent and kind.

Keep up the good work.

Te mata Peak

Everyday courage has few witnesses. But yours is no less noble because no drum beats before you and no crowds shout your name.

– Robert Louis Stevenson

Te Mata Peak is a mountain in Hawke's Bay, about twenty minutes' drive from where my wife and I have our health and fitness centre in New Zealand. It's an amazing place with beautiful scenery and also awesome energy. The energy there is mind-blowing.

One evening my friend Michael and I went to the top of the peak. It was dark and it was just lit by the moonlight and the stars. We both had an urge to go up there to see what and who we could communicate with.

At the top of the peak there are two rocks, with a male and a female energy. Michael stood on one and I stood on the other. We stood there looking down into the valley as far as the moonlight would let us. What happened next was amazing. St Germain, one of the ascended masters who has reached a level in spiritual growth that is immense, came to talk to us. He is in many places at once helping and guiding many human beings on their own journeys. He has touched the hearts of many, for centuries, and will continue to do so in the present, regardless of the time and space it's in. I believe his aim is to enlighten as many of the human race as possible. Those who are ready to know the truth will be accelerated on their journeys by communicating with this perfect being of light.

St Germain is well known for the violet flame, which is used to a powerful and positive effect. For any of you that desire more knowledge please look into St Germain yourself and you will, from experience, be graced with his presence at some point, not too far away, as long as you are ready – only you can answer this question.

As Michael and I stood their meditating in our own ways St Germain came into my conscious mind and spoke to me. He asked me to follow him. As I followed him in my mind I was speaking to Michael, who stood about seven to eight metres away on the other rock. He could see what I was seeing. He saw exactly where St Germain wanted to take us.

Together we walked forward and were taken down a creamy stone, spiral staircase. As we walked down and down and round and round the energy of his presence was electrifying. As we got to the bottom of the stairs there was a door. We walked through the door and into a room. A group of children were huddled up on the floor. They had dark skin and looked hungry and afraid. They were prisoners and Michael and I had been asked to free them. With our minds we focused on letting them go and a hole appeared in the side of the wall. It was more like a part of the wall had been removed. We told the children not to be afraid, to go and be free. They got up and left.

On the outside of the room was a beautiful river, the sun was shining and it was like we were in the jungle somewhere. The kids ran away, happy and content that their suffering had ended. Both Michael and I were told a few days later when we sat channelling with St Germain that he had been trying to get us both back together for sixty thousand years. This could be another reason I ended up in New Zealand; I think so.

We are both on a mission to shine light and spread the word and help humanity return to its former glory. Michael is about sixty years of age but has the energy of a twenty year old, an amazing man, human being and dear friend. We are both at present on separate paths which are a part of the bigger picture, so really on the same path and I know very soon our paths will cross again as there is much work to do.

My life is engaged in freeing people from their individual troubles and my mission as a spiritual warrior is to help each and every human being, rediscover the truth and help them become aware of truth in all things. When St Germain showed me these children and their suffering this was a test – I could have carried on moving and let them be but I didn't; I set them free to explore and live the rest of their lives, free as little birds, the way it should be.

I have been tested and passed my tests and as I pass each one I become stronger, both mentally, physically and more importantly spiritually and as I do I am entrusted with more work to do. Hence the writing of this book and the engagement of the fairies and angels in the communication to help me channel these messages.

Do all that you can each day to be kind and considerate to your fellow human beings. Do all that you can to unlock the minds of men and women. Lead by example and never force yourself on others. Lead by example and inspire them to want to get to know you, and follow you in your footsteps, as you light the way for others and encourage them to start their spiritual journeys.

Going Back Home

First say to yourself what would you be,
and then do what you have to do.

– **Epictetus**

Do you think that we are the only life force in the solar system? Did you think that Earth is the only planet that has a living community?

If you did, think again. There are many planets out there in this vast galaxy and there are many with different life forces inhabiting them. We call them aliens. Why? They are not aliens; they are just different from you or I. They actually care about us and the thought of an alien invasion is a nonstarter. I have talked about Mother Earth being dense and that we need to raise our vibration as a global community in order to rise up and into the light.

If we do not, not that this is going to happen because we have so much support from other beings of light, in many shapes and forms, we could possibly go into darkness and end up like Atlantis, thousands of years ago. As I said it's a nonstarter, so no need to worry. I promise you we will rise into the light once and for all and stay there.

If Mother Earth and her beloved inhabitants could not raise the vibration however, it would affect not only our planet but every other planet across the galaxy. A ripple effect could have the capability of tipping other planets out of balance also. This is important as it should give you some extra reassurance, that every other life force that exists wants us human beings to raise our vibration and just like the angels, fairies and other special beings of light, beings from other planets are assisting us too.

I don't like to call them aliens. Maybe we are the aliens. After all we are just as alien to them as they are to us. I am standing in my truth here and now divulging this information; however, it's my duty to inform you and let you know, of the magnitude and careful preparation that's taking place throughout the entire system, to ensure our safety and victory.

Extraterrestrials are shown to us in films to desensitise us from being shocked when the time comes for them to reveal themselves to us, and they will. I cannot wait. What a glorious moment it will be. They are also shown to us as scary or nasty creatures that would want to abduct us and cause us harm. This is total garbage. They care for us humans in a way in which you cannot imagine.

Extraterrestrial life forms have been around longer than the human race. We are a young race compared to them. I was originally from a planet system called Alpha Centuria. They were very connected to the human race at one time. However, over the centuries they have developed much faster than the human race. I travelled there not so long ago during a meditation inside my friend's pyramid. Copper pyramids, if built correctly and placed at certain nautical points, allow energy to flow and the mind to wander more freely. My friend Michael has one in his garden. I have spent many hours sitting inside it meditating and letting my mind be taken to interesting and exciting places.

I was sitting there one day breathing and relaxing my mind and I saw what I would describe as a space pod land next to me in the garden. A humanoid looking being, with intense but friendly energy, asked me to get inside. So I took my light and jumped inside the vehicle. We travelled at speeds I cannot describe and landed on Alpha Centuria, my home planet from many years ago. As I stepped out of the aircraft my feet felt the ground and it was warm. I needed a pair of shades as it was that bright. There were many beings there to welcome me, as though I had arrived home after a long holiday. I felt so at home and at peace.

The technology on this planet far supersedes that of the human race and each being had shades that just appeared and disappeared as they needed them. They were taller than I was, maybe six and a half to seven feet tall with a greyish skin colour. They had little or no hair at all on their bodies and all were in good shape. They only consumed that which is necessary for their life and never overindulged like many of us human beings, here on Earth.

The planet was beautiful, colourful, with streams and forests and no apparent environmental issues. It really seemed like paradise. I stayed for a short while and they introduced me to their chief. That is the only way I can recall the introduction. Like you see in films when someone is introduced to an Indian tribal leader. It was exhilarating.

When it was time to leave we jumped back in the space pod and within seconds had travelled millions of miles back to Michael's garden. What a rush. That's all I can say.

Another time I was in the pyramid and my feet turned to balls of fire and Jesus came and stood in front of me. He said that I can walk anywhere I want with confidence and then he vanished and left me looking at a huge wooden door. As I walked up to it and then through it I was in a room; there were a group of men sitting round a large table eating a feast. Jesus was at the end of the table giving a speech. I was in the room. It was a past life experience I was being shown, one I had not previously been privy to.

I was Matthew, one of the twelve disciples and Jesus was giving his last supper speech. It was so surreal. I have heard the story many times but to be an actual part of it was strange but amazing at the same time. I looked out of a window in the room and I saw a space ship. It was ginormous. It was a message to let me know that all the way back then, just in case I had any doubts and needed confirmation that beings of light, from other planets, were amongst us, guiding and assisting the path of us human beings to ensure our earthly life was taking a good shape.

I was back in my body minutes later, slumped in a chair in the pyramid, astounded at what had just happened.

Fellow warriors of light, I am sharing this with you to give you confidence to grow and rise up from where you are stood at this present moment. You have the power within you to remember your past lives and other planetary homes, where once you took refuge. So much knowledge is locked away in your subconscious mind and all you have to do is start asking questions. Meditate as often as you can. At least, once a day. Short periods of time and build up as you feel you are ready.

We must find balance and a part of this balance is to give time back to ourselves to rest, play and explore our minds. Soon we will be communicating telepathically and when we do our lives will be full of happiness and prosperity, in all areas. I cannot wait for this day. I am exercising my patience, a big challenge for me in this lifetime, until we reach this glorious moment.

Be happy that there is more to life than what you can see, touch, taste, smell or hear. Soon, as your vibration rises, you too will have access to all the files, the information contained in your soul. You will unlock many memories, pure and happy memories that will take you to wonderful places of understanding and readiness. You are being prepared for an amazing transformation, one where you will be living the most perfect life, the life you knew you were destined to live before you came down into this earthly bodily to live as a human being. One with a life goal, to fulfil a dream and banish all negativity, from this earthly plane and bring the world and its global community back together in peace, love and harmony once again.

Acceptance, Judgement or Responsibility

What if we should discover that the poorest of beggars
and the most impudent of offenders are all within me, and
that I stand in need of the alms of my own kindness; that I
myself am the enemy who must be loved – what then?

– Carl Jung

This journey through life tests us, shapes us, and moulds us into the human beings we are. We must be grateful for every opportunity to grow spiritually. Quite often when we are tested by others it's for our own benefit. When incidents happen or circumstances don't go our way, we are learning valuable lessons about who we are, what makes us tick and how to deal with it so as to avoid the situation again.

Throughout your life as you travel your journey, there will be many occasions where you will be tested and in many different ways. Regardless of what tests you face, hurdles you must overcome or mountains you must navigate, you must always, no matter what, take responsibility for yourself.

Remember, you are creating your own Universe as you travel through time and everything that is happening around you is the results of your thoughts, feelings and actions. You can never blame another human being for what is happening around you, even if they have done something wrong at a particular time. Remember you have created the situation and have to take responsibility yourself. It may be that you attracted that person into your life, to make a mistake, to give you a chance to deal with this particular situation effectively. It may be that this person works for you and you may have to let them go; however, that will be to both of your benefits as you will both be learning extremely valuable lessons. Everything is perfect as it is.

Everything is always perfect as it is, as long as you can accept the person or the situation and not look for excuses or reasons why it has happened or look to blame another for this lesson you are supposed to be learning.

You need to learn to never judge another human being. Full acceptance is the order of the day. I know it can be hard as we are patterned to carry judgement from a young age. I remember my parents would always judge others they knew and others they didn't. They would judge their appearance, financial status, and attitude. There were all sorts of reasons; they still do it to this day. I just smile and take my mind to another place of enjoyment and happiness as they criticise or reduce others for whatever reason they have built up in their minds without knowing the truth. As human beings living in this time and space, where the ego is in full control of a lot of minds right now, we put labels on everything.

These labels allow us to identify other people and/or situations and we even label ourselves. The labelling of self is also an identity mechanism; it's who we truly believe we are. The truth of the matter is, however, that it's all an illusion. We conceptualize everything and see life and what we deem to be reality, through a pair of rose tinted glasses. Once we reconnect with our inner spirit, this identifying with oneself and others through the thought patterns of the ego, disappear, once and for all.

We must accept everyone for who they are. Remember they are learning lessons on their own personal journey too. None of us know what is for the greatest good of each individual's growth and spiritual development. Let nature take its course and let each and every human being be as they are. The best thing you can do is to lead by example. Do your own thing and let everyone know why you are so happy. You are happy because you have found the truth and so too can they. As long as they look in the most important place on earth, inside themselves, for the answers, knowledge and priceless information.

The ego labels all situations, events and people, and this is harmful. The ego creates its own identity, and in turn the identity you perceive to be right, by labelling and judging others and also yourself. Please stop this at once. Everyone is perfect as they are; you are no different. Even those human beings who are totally ruled by their ego, and cause harm to others, through conflict, war and other so-called evil deeds. We are all learning and each and every one of us is at a different level, in the game. It's a huge philosophical game of one life, and we are all tiny players on the board.

Life is full of lessons, good and not so good but they all make you stronger and you grow from each one; as long as you, the real and internal you, accept each one and take responsibility knowing that you created the situation for your own personal growth. Life is so perfect; nothing is ever out of place. It may seem like it is at the present time when the event is taking place around you, but if you stay calm, relax and just take it in your stride you will see that there is a reason why. It may not be apparent immediately but it will become clear; it's inevitable as long as you stay calm and accept the situation, the Universe, your Genie, will provide you with the answers to the questions you have, regarding the particular lesson at hand.

I have been in situations myself and I know others who have also. Business situations or deals you could be working on may fall apart at the seams for no apparent reason. You put your time and effort into it and inexplicably it goes belly up. The important thing to do in this situation is to stay calm and be grateful.

You are perfect, life is perfect and everything in your life is perfect, even where you are right now. It's perfect for this time and space. You had to be where you are right now to progress in the way in which your life has unfolded. We all have a path and our job is to focus and stay on that path. Sometimes we make a wrong turn but your Genie will always guide you back through your thoughts and feelings and awareness of your surroundings. Be open and listen.

Take responsibility and accept every situation for what it really is – a lesson – and you will detoxify your soul of any potential worries or fears that could have risen from the situation you are dealing with. You will be at peace once you realise and accept everything as being perfect and you will see only true perfection in your life and it will unfold naturally around you with ease. You will feel fantastic all of the time. Your mind, body and soul will be in perfect harmony with the Universe and life will get better and better and better. That's my promise to you.

You may have suffered a serious injury, which left you without the use of your legs. Accept this as a part of your journey and then you will have a chance of regaining the use out of them. Miracles can take place. The human mind, if used the right way can rebuild nerves, muscle, tissue and put back together what was once a broken body. If you get angry at the situation and feel sorry for yourself you will only add stress and complicate your mind with fears and emotions that are harmful. Let go and free yourself, connect with source, the powerful energy that created you and open the door, once again, to your creative centre, as from this place all magic happens and all possibilities are available.

Regardless of how horrific a situation may seem, acceptance is the key. Acceptance leads to awareness and total connection with spirit. It's here that you will harness your power, your true power, the power that will let you live and not merely exist. You can be in a prison cell, locked away and still be free. A man or woman sitting at home in their million dollar mansion, locked in the prison of their mind, jailed by the non-accepting conditioning of life is in a harsher environment than a man or woman locked in a prison cell, twenty three hours a day, knowing they are in there for life, but who has journeyed back to where they originally came from. They have chosen the path of love and light and accepted all of life for what it is, now, in this moment and have connected with the reality of the true essence, of the human being they really are.

'The Kingdom of heaven is within' – Jesus

Healthy Mind

Small doubt, small enlightenment. Great doubt, great enlightenment.

– Zen saying

The mind is so powerful and in terms of health or ill health, the mind plays its role, in creating and manifesting the so called illness or disease, and if the mind is free, a perfectly healthy body.

People tell me they have this problem and this issue and/or need this operation and when they look to me for sympathy and I tell them it's all in their mind, and that they can sort it out without a doctor, medicine or operation, they look at me like I have gone mad.

Doctors and hospitals do have their place, however, for serious incidents. I won't say accidents because I don't believe there are any accidents – everything happens for a reason. If you get run over by a car emergency treatment may be needed and could potentially save your life, so everything has its place. We have to be aware, however, of where the boundaries of these uses lie. Your new-found awareness will steer you in the right direction.

My friends will say to me, 'But it actually hurts you know', 'Can you not see this lump?' 'The doctor says this' or 'the doctor says that'. I am not suggesting for one minute that the problem doesn't exist and it's a figment of their imagination, but what I am stating is the fact that this problem can be resolved, with a shift in emotions or thought patterns. Illness or injury is a concept in the mind.

Let me give you an example of an injury I was faced with. One day I was training at the gym and my left shoulder started aching and as the weeks went by I got weaker and the pain was more intense. I went to see a doctor and had scans, I had acupuncture, physiotherapy, massage therapy and a bunch of other treatments. None of them worked. Everyone had their own personal opinion but the problem just would not go away.

A year had gone past by this point and my training had suffered a lot. Two very good friends of mine were physiotherapists and had been studying the link between the mind and the body, and had started treating their patients without ever touching them. I went to see them, and they asked me a series of questions.

To cut a long story short it turned out that I was annoyed at a guy I had working for me. After careful consideration to ensure I was doing the right thing, I decided I would ask this person to leave my company. The strangest thing happened. As soon as I made the conscious decision to ask him to leave, my Genie presented an opportunity that made it easy for me to ask him to leave. He did something wrong and I caught him in the act and so the dismissal was easy.

The other thing that happened was that as soon as I made the conscious decision, to ask him to leave, my shoulder felt much better. Within twenty four hours it was as good as new. My negative thoughts over the course of time had manifested themselves inside my shoulder and turned into an injury that could only be fixed by the removal of that energy. My conscious decision to let my employee go, resulted in that energy moving on and my shoulder being restored to good as new.

The power of thought had attracted the problem but also released it, and also created an easy dismissal. Your mind and your thoughts really are that strong. You are amazing, we all are, but just as your thoughts can create harmony and bliss and a rich and fruitful life, full of health and love, so can your thoughts create illness and disease.

I am going to share with you a story about a friend of mine, Trish; she is like an angel, a real life angel. This particular angel helped me so much in my life. Here I had a chance to give something back.

One day Trish was involved in a near-fatal car accident and ended up in hospital in intensive care. The hospital had her on so much morphine that she could not use her senses properly and her ability to heal herself with the use of her mind was lessened.

I had a call from her partner one day and she asked me to help fix her. Every rib had been smashed and she was struggling to breathe. I was in New Zealand at the time and she was laid up in hospital in Bristol, England.

I am telling you this story as I want you to understand the power of the mind and how it can be applied to yourself and/or others, to help in healing.

So I lay down on my bed and focused every bit of energy I could summon and took myself into her hospital room, sat by her bed and focused an array of different healing colours onto her body and mentally started putting her ribs back together. I spent hours, every day, for weeks, doing this. The doctors told her she would be in hospital for a long time and may never walk again.

Also at this time, Trish was having trouble with a man, from another realm, who kept coming into her room and bothering her. Again she was too weak to stop him so I went in and asked him to leave. I put triangular shapes of light, across every wall. Four triangles in all, on every wall, the flat side on the outsides of the wall and the points all met in the middle. I then sealed them after with my mind and covered them in light and it stopped this gentleman entering and bothering her again.

When focusing my energy on Trish I would use my ray of light. We all have one and are capable of using it to heal, to send love, to travel and manifest the most marvellous life as long as the ray is used for the right reasons, for light and not dark. To use my ray I lie down flat with my eyes closed. I take a few deep breaths, empty my mind, centre myself and then see the ray of light coming from my base chakra. It is different colours, but mainly white or violet. I will send the ray from my body to wherever it needs to travel to and in this case to Trish's body inside her hospital room. In my mind I was sat next to her bed. I could describe the room as clear as day.

Once I sat next to her and used my ray from my body to heal her; I also used rays from my hands to focus in on small points on her body, such as the ribs. One by one I mentally put the shape back together again and sealed them with light. This allowed her to breathe more easily as the ribs were pressing on her lungs and were terribly painful. I continued to work across Trish's body and slowly put her back together again. This power is not unique. It's within us all. It must be remembered and re-developed. Like anything, practice makes perfect.

Trish recovered, and was out of hospital in twelve weeks and she walked out. The power of the mind healed her physically, in no time at all.

What was interesting for me was once Trish came out of hospital and I got to speak to her, she told me that one night she opened her eyes and looked at the side of her bed and said, 'What are you doing here?' She was talking to me. I had imagined myself in her hospital bed, working on her with my ray of light, my energy and my mind, and in actual fact, in spirit, I had transported myself into her room and was actually sat by her bed. She saw me as clear as day.

I want you to know how powerful we all are. I am not different from you or anyone else in this world. We all have the capabilities to use our minds to heal ourselves and others. You just have to be aware and trust yourself to explore and try it for yourself.

Be brave, don't be afraid to experiment and see what works for you. I remember when I first realised the potential of our minds – I took a headache out of my wife's head. Sounds a bit crazy but this is what I did.

She had a really nasty migraine and was lying on the floor. I sat next to her and placed my hand on her head. I focused my mind on the energy inside her that was causing her to have the headache and then gradually I lifted my hand away from her head. I could see the energy lifting with my hand and after about ten minutes of doing this her headache had gone. It had vanished totally. She had been in a place where she could not move or open her eyes. But within minutes she was up and moving around like she had never had a headache in the first place.

Believe you can do the same and you will.

Don't forget you are amazing, a being of infinite potential and you have the capability to do anything you want with your life, including healing yourself and others.

I want to give you one more example. My son Josh had asthma as a young child. Well he still is young, he's only eight, but it seems like lifetimes ago now. When he was two years of age, the doctors gave him an inhaler. He had been rushed to hospital a few times. I remember sitting by his bedside praying he would pull through. Now, for a few years we would get up each day and give him his inhaler as standard practice and his asthma never got better. There were times when it was better than others, but ultimately it was still there.

One day my wife Laura said, 'That's it, I am chucking the inhaler in the bin. Nothing else seems to be working. Maybe he's not getting better because we wake up every day and give him the inhaler and so his mind thinks it needs to produce the symptoms of asthma, wheezing etc.'

So Laura threw away the inhaler and we stopped talking about it. We didn't ask Josh, our son, how he was feeling anymore. It was pretty much immediate, maybe within a week or less – he stopped wheezing. No more asthma. He wasn't taking the inhaler anymore so his mind assumed he was better and so his body no longer produced the symptoms of someone having asthma.

You see, illness is a concept created by the human mind and can be dissolved just as quickly as it was created. Every disease can be taken care of by focusing your attention on the opposite, and that is that there is only perfect health and a state of internal perfection. This will create health and beauty on the outside also.

Let's talk about emotions.

We all have barriers and boundaries that act as imaginary controlling factors in our lives. They keep us pinned down or penned in. Life gives us opportunities to break down these barriers. Opportunity gives us the chance to stretch and expand our lives, and in doing so we dissolve the boundaries ingrained in our minds, patterns that have been sewn into our belief systems from a young age.

As we grow and are patterned by what we see, hear, smell, feel, taste and touch we develop an identity of who we are. Our patterning can often happen in the first seven years of our lives. We feel many emotions and develop a variety of behavioural patterns, many of which do not serve us well and in the end can make us ill. When we are born we are born into purity. We are born with no judgement, hatred, anger, jealousy or any other conceptualisations and identity-making mechanisms that we create. As we grow we begin to label everything when life doesn't need any labels at all. There is an intelligence at work that is greater than you or I. This intelligence is in everything and so things do not need names. Everything boils down to emotions and in turn our feelings, and when you look very closely you will see that anything in life that does not serve us is underpinned by one defining factor. That factor is fear.

When we were born we were free, happy and full of love, with no pains, ailments or disease. We had no concepts of life and the way it should be etched into our minds. As we grow in life we become more detached from these core and true feelings. Layers and layers of toxic waste are stored around what is true. That truth is that we are loving, kind and compassionate human beings that want the best for ourselves and everyone else.

If you can imagine there is the real you on the inside and the conceptual you on the outside and in-between are these layers of toxic, acidic feelings and emotions that instil a number of limiting belief systems and our task is to strip away the layers until we find our truth once more. Just like peeling back the layers on an onion until the bare centrepiece, the purity, is left in the middle.

What is holding these toxic emotions in place? Fear. When you get to the core of the matter, it's fear that encourages these unexpressed emotions and in turn the emotions instil limiting beliefs and behaviour patterns into our lives. When we experience a stressful event in our lives an imprint, much like a stamp, is pressed into our system on four different levels. There is an intellectual imprint in our memory, a chemical imprint produced by hormones that are released into the body, a visual imprint in the subconscious mind and the fourth being on a cellular or energetic level.

Bodily hormones have a lifespan after being injected into the cells, much like milk does in your fridge. Once they go off they become toxic and can cause pain or illness in the body. It's important that we accept and honour our emotions by expressing them and in turn allowing the toxins to leave the body. According to medical records eighty five percent of illness is stress related and doctors now have a stress injection to cure it. This has to be the biggest money-making con and mind controlling remedy I have ever heard of. Especially when all we need to do is to accept, honour and release our emotions.

It's our duty to humanity to send out this message and let everyone else in the world know, that they have been born with infinite potential to create the very existence you and I know how to live.

This includes a perfectly, healthy, strong, young, flexible body.

Waking Up

In a dark time, the eye begins to see.

– Theodore Roethke

This whole experience is about waking up and becoming aware. Each and every human being is engaging with others who, like you and I, think outside of the box and think and act in a way in which everyone benefits.

Society as a whole is waking up. More and more, day by day, the global community in which we live is becoming aware of what lies outside the reality we are forced to believe as being real. Well this reality is becoming extinct in the mind of awakened human beings. The rate at which the word spreads will pick up steam. Acceleration is the operating force right now. The grand master element of eternal love is pressing his foot hard on the accelerator and no other force is strong enough to compete with that of the force of love, so that foot will keep on pressing until we reach our final destination, that of peace and tranquillity.

Are you as excited as I am? This is so cool. So many beings of light are awake right now, that the once-strong force of darkness that existed and ruled will evaporate into thin air to become a fairytale of its own. However, it will be a fairytale never talked of as our energies will not focus upon that which we do not want.

We will centre ourselves in joy and contentment and relish in this vast and open land, that we can now call the land of the free. For once it has happened we will never step back in time. We will be focused and thoughtful and ensure our elegant and powerful thought forces only process those thoughts of passion and harmony.

We will be returning to spirit, knowing that our mission was accomplished and we won the battle at hand. We will forever live with a sparkle in our eyes and love in our hearts, because we deserve that and more. We deserve abundance; it's our birthright after all. The knowledge that we possess gives us total opportunity to develop our skill base and use the most powerful tool that we possess to go out and create the life we so rightly want and deserve. Love, health and money in abundance are calling you. Create it, it's yours. Decide, like I did, that you will change from this day forward and lead the way.

Become the being of light you know in your heart of hearts you can be. Climb the ladder and help all others up behind you. Carve a path for all who desire and dream the reality of peace, joy and happiness, to follow with ease. Let's rise together as one glorified unit, completing the mission that others before us had started. We are so lucky. We are in this time and space right now and we are going to live and see first-hand, the outcome, the inevitable result of light workers' work for many centuries before us.

Be proud. I know I am; you should be so too. As I look down upon you from heaven above, I can see the internal smile in your heart radiating pure and utter excitement, and so you should. It's a golden time for all of humanity.

Fearless

If you feel any fear at all by moving in one particular direction, know this. Move in that direction. Your largest life, the life of your dreams, always lives on the other side of your fears.

– Jerry Sargeant

No more ego. This is your goal. When I say goal, you must not see this as a future goal. If you see it as a future goal it will always remain in the future. See it as real, as something that's taken place. Your ego is 100% fear-based. Fear fuels your ego and if you had no fear the ego would have nothing to nourish itself and so fade away and become non-existent.

The ego tries to control you and keep you living in fear, but there really is nothing to be fearful of. Fear is created within and so can be dissolved within. You do not need to live your life on a knife edge because you fear all the things that could go wrong. Why not think about all the things that could go right, in every situation, and strip the life force of the ego? If you do, you will feel magnificent.

Just as the lady on the plane's ego was trying to stop her from sitting next to me, so are other human beings' egos holding them back on their own personal journeys and keeping them bogged down in this dense and heavy existence, here on Mother Earth.

My mission is to rid the human race of their ego and show them that there is nothing at all to fear. Fear really is an illusion, an imaginary barrier, created in your own mind, by your ego, to stop you from moving forward in life, towards your goals and your dreams.

When we incarnate into our bodies we know that it will be a struggle at times to stay on track, on the path and fulfil our mission. When we stray off track the Universe guides us back. Sometimes, however, we are in such a dark place that we cannot listen, accept or take on board the necessary help. I myself was in a place like that, but the angry old man came to my rescue, with the help of my beautiful wife, who was more open and lighter in her vibration than I was.

If we can inspire others to follow in our footsteps, they too can benefit from the guidance from above and all around us. It's offered free of charge. Why would we not want the help? We know its perfect guidance, in real time, to ensure we are full of love, success, happiness and are having endless amounts of fun.

There will come a time when we all communicate telepathically again, just like on Atlantis and Lemuria. When this happens there will be no more fear or lies. The truth is only hidden right now because we are allowed to plainly ignore our internal guidance system, our gut instinct, that always knows what's best. When we start to communicate again, like the ways of old, we will no longer be faced with this issue. If I think something, you will hear it, so nothing goes unnoticed.

How amazing will it be to have no more lies, white lies or denial of the right path to follow?

Let's take the ego out of this world, once and for all. Let's be all that we can be. Others will see your accomplishments and want to follow where you boldly went. They will be enlightened by your presence without you having to speak a word. You can remain in silence, going about your daily work, knowing you are a walking beacon of light and soon each and every living soul, around you on this planet, will also be walking with you side by side, vibrating at the same frequency as you.

Heaven, here we come.

Installing Faith

A dreamer is one who can only find his way by moonlight, and his punishment is that he sees the dawn before the rest of the world.

– Oscar Wilde

It's very important that you believe in everything that you do, wholeheartedly, without a shadow of doubt entering your mind. You can choose, very easily, by making a conscious decision, to believe in yourself and never again return to the mind that is ruled by fear, and inevitably, the mind that casts doubt on your actions.

I know (as I have seen it already) that you are destined for success and amazing things are about to unfold in your life. You are about to become enlightened, blessed and driven to fulfil the goals and dreams that once seemed out of reach. You have woken up and life is treating you with the respect you so rightly deserve – isn't it wonderful? A shift in your awareness, since you have been reading this, has changed the course of your life.

I am looking down on you now, dear child, with amazement at how far you have come on your spiritual journey. Your belief is growing and your faith is getting stronger and stronger. I want to give you some extra tools that will aid you, to ensure that the faith, deep in your soul, fuels your every thought and the energy inside of you will get stronger by the day, instilling you and your internal guidance system with a faith so pure that any potential obstacle will melt away at your feet, as you move towards it, never again will you have a second thought. Just one thought, followed through by action, guided by a desire to do good and driven by a faith so strong and pure.

Wow, you really are special.

I want you to start a daily practice that will accelerate your forward movement and collectively add to the global benefit of the greater good of all mankind. The more focused you become the faster the results. The more effort you put into achieving greatness the faster others will follow in your footsteps.

Each morning when you awake I would like you to start daily mediation. If you can't make it work in the morning then pick a time during your day that you can spend fifteen minutes, in a quiet space, relaxing your mind and letting your energy flow. You need to close your eyes, breathe deeply and empty your mind of any of the daily thoughts you would normally be thinking. It takes practice and the more you do it the easier it will become.

Once your mind is clear, ask yourself questions and the first thought that comes into your mind will be the answer from your guides, higher self or the Universe. Listen carefully with a relaxed mind and don't try and force the answers. Once you are relaxed enough and we feel that you are ready, your guides will present themselves to you in your mind's eye. This may take some time. We are all different so, please, do not stress if it takes weeks or months – it will, however, happen.

Your guides are with you at all times; they always have been and always will be, so feel safe in their presence. They are your friends, allies of the spirit world, a part of the great force that is protecting this planet and once you see them you will be enlightened to heights that I cannot explain in words.

Daily meditation will help you connect to source and open the channels of communication. You can also visualise during this process. Please focus on the world living in peace and harmony, a new earth that is blessed with kindness and all ill feelings and thoughts of others have disappeared into the distance, swallowed up by the force of love and forever lost in the beauty of this new and peaceful world.

During your visualisation, focus on your life and what you would like it to be like. Focus on everything that you want. Your aims, goals and dreams and live your new life out in your mind as though it was your actual reality, in this time and space. Be grateful, thank the Universe for this new life, as though everything you are thinking about at that moment is a tangible possession or pure feeling of contentment.

To stimulate your faith and communicate directly with your subconscious mind, I also want you to go into a daily practice of saying affirmations in your mind. An affirmation is a sentence, a string of words, created to cement whatever it is that you desire, deep inside your mind. Affirmations are like planting the seeds of true and pure thoughts that will, very soon, spring into action and grow into beautiful flowers in the garden of your mind. You can choose the flowers, trees and plants that grow. No longer do you have to accept a weed-ridden garden, over-run by the thoughts installed by the world news stations.

From now on you do not give any outside influence or third party the chance to embed the patterns of corruption and distress into your mind. Now you will start and conclude every day with affirmations that will increase your desire and faith. During each day you will remain focused on that which you want, seeing the truth in all things.

You can design your own affirmations but here is a small list that you can utilise. It will start you on the right road and then you can build upon the list. Once you complete one affirmation and it is engrained within your soul, you can move on to the next one you need to work on or you may want to have several affirmations running at the same time. I have ones I religiously do and will always do and others that come and go.

When you say your affirmations please do them in groups of eleven. If you say one affirmation, say it eleven times. You must say each affirmation eleven times and for a period of fifty five days. If you skip a day you must go back and start again. You can say each affirmation twenty two or thirty three times for faster effects, but maintain the fifty five day process to properly cement it, deep within subconscious.

Here is a list you can use to get on with:

- I am happy at all times and my life is magically unfolding in the perfect way.

- My life is full of happiness and joy and I have much love myself and every other human being.

- I have perfect health and my mind is clear and content as I proceed on my spiritual journey.

- I have an abundance of love, health and money in my life. I am fulfilled and everything I need comes to me with ease.

- I am safe, secure, protected and supported by my light at all times. (This is one I have said daily for many years)

- There is only good and happiness in the world we live in and my spirit guides are lighting my path every single day.

- The world is full of love.

- I am connected to source, and have willingly opened all channels of communication, with all light beings involved in our mission to bring peace and joy to the world.

- I am living in prosperity and will lead by example as I create my own perfect life.

- I am happy and feel positivity to others at all times.

This list will get you started and give you an idea of how you can build and develop your own list, dependent on your goals, desires and dreams.

Release It

The beauty of the soul shines out when a person bears with composure one mischance after another, not because he does not feel them, but because he is one of high and heroic temper.

– Unknown

We are at a stage here on Mother Earth where technology is at the forefront of life. For most, we have televisions, computers, and radios and are engrossed in the world news stations and many other forms of media, such as newspapers and magazines.

Most human beings wake up, turn on the TV or radio and listen to it whilst getting ready in the morning, I cannot think of a more horrifying way to start the day. How about a little walk, or jog or maybe some light yoga?

The thoughts that place in a mind ruled by ego are mostly of a negative nature. The ego labels everything you see, people, events, circumstances, even you. Labels are stuck on everything. Life is put into boxes and conceptualized. The ego puts thoughts of jealousy, fear and judgement into your mind. It's time to release them all.

If we, as a human race, want to wake up and give ourselves the best possible chance of survival then we need to do everything in our power to give us the best chance of success. When was the last time you switched on the news and it made you happy, because of the amazing story that was screened before your very eyes?

That's what I thought: you couldn't recall one. All we are shown is not so good news. This is the reason I threw my TV away in 2008. We watch the odd DVD now and again on the computer, but that's it. The difference it makes to our lives is immense and in a positive fashion. People mention the news to me and I have not got a clue what they are talking about. To be honest, why would I want to know? It doesn't serve me, my family or friends or any other beautiful human being for that matter, so why would I even entertain a conversation with a topic of not so good news.

I am trying to dissolve my egoic mind in its entirety and filling my mind with negative images will just fuel the ego and help bring back the old pattering, and it will make a play and try and over-run my mind, leading my thoughts astray and down a path that will end in misery, guaranteed.

The technological age can be of benefit, however. If more TV shows were produced that discussed the very topic that I am discussing with you, here in this book, it would be worth tuning into. What you have to remember is that many of those who are in control do not want these kind of messages coming out. They do not want the world to find peace in their hearts. They want the world to live in fear so they can be controlled. This is changing slowly though.

Many human beings who work in television, radio and other forms of media are being contacted by beings of light. Human beings, just like you and me, who have woken up and are on a mission to bring back the power to each and every human being on this planet. It is happening all over the world and the more we spread this message the better, the faster humanity will wake up as a collective and once it reaches tipping point, when more than fifty percent of the population discover the truth, there will be no stopping it.

We are not far off. Just focus on you for now. Re-connect with your inner child, your inner self, the being of light that you are and raise your own conscious awareness to heights of clarity that will give you the clear vision you need, to let the love spill out into the world.

Keep your mind focused on what is important and that is you. Do not feed your mind and soul with images that will be detrimental to your goals of achieving inner peace. Once you find this peace your life will magically change. You will no longer need anything to make you happy, because true happiness lies within. I want you to know, however, that you deserve a fruitful life and you have the capability to achieve one. A life full of health, love and money. What you must remember, however, is that the life you desire must be acquired so you can live a maximum life, and not because you are looking to satisfy your needs and wants. There's only one place that will happen, and it's inside you. It's been there all along.

You deserve everything you can have, to enjoy and have fun with, as a human being living in this time and space, but you must not go after anything, whether it's love, health or money, to simply make you feel good. The only thing that can make you feel good is connecting with your inner awareness, bringing through the light that lies within, and letting the love shine though and consume your mind, body and soul.

Out Of or Into the World

Only those who risk going too far can possibly find out how far one can go.

– T. S. Eliot

So were you born into this world or were you born out of this world? Are you a victim of the world or are you the world?

As children we say to our parents, who made me or how was I made? It's a common misconception, derived from our upbringing, that we believe we were made and that someone made us. We were not made; nature itself by the mere fact that it's natural, implies that it must have evolved and grown from somewhere and that it was not made.

Are we made or are we natural? The answer is we are natural beings that grew out from somewhere. But where? We grew out of a formless substance, a creative force that all things in this Universe have grown out of, and will continue to grow out of. We are like apples growing out on the branches of an apple tree, not birds that have taken refuge on an old dead tree. We are a part of the Universe and in being a part of the Universe are a part of the whole, the entire world we know and live in.

Many human beings think we are bones, muscles, organs, blood and all the other things that make up our body, held together by a bag of skin, and that everything on the outside of this is something else, that there is an in here and an out there. If you look at the world through a microscope, the naked eye or a telescope, which view is the correct view? Well it turns out that they are all correct, just different viewpoints.

If you look at a photograph of a girl in a newspaper, with the naked eye, then what you see is a girl. If you see the same photograph through a microscope you will see lots of tiny dots, and as you move further away these tiny dots become the photograph again. The entire world, all objects, people, animals and all other creatures great and small are exactly the same. This mass of energy makes up the entire system. Dots and lots of space.

There is not an in here or an out there. You cannot have an inside without having an outside. You would not see the object if there was no background, behind it or surrounding it. It would just become one, so the inside and the outside are inherently linked. So in essence the inside and the outside must be a part of the same thing, a part of the whole, the Universe as one.

You cannot have an inside without an outside, and you cannot have an outside without an inside or everything would be one complete vision and inseparable to the naked eye. In fact all things are separable when you put them under a high powered microscope and it is in fact one complete vision, regardless of whether you look through a microscope, the naked eye or a telescope.

You see there is space all around us and space that makes up everything in the Universe. There is space in our bodies and space in and through all matter. Atoms and molecules in continuous motion and lots of space is the energy, the essence of the Universe, the formless substance that makes up all things. It is all things. Energy is always moving through form and out of form and is in continuous motion. The flame on a candle is burning gas and the shape you see of a burring candle in a dark room, flickering away, is simply a pattern. To the eye it looks like a flame, that's what we call it, but it's just energy, continuously moving and creating the pattern of what we call a flame. Human beings are the same. Today I am Jerry Sargeant. Next week, I will still be the pattern of Jerry Sargeant but my body will be a complete make up of different energy, that's moved through form and out of form and back into form again. Energy is constantly moving and so my body today and my body next week will have new atoms and molecules and space making it up and enabling other human beings to see me, as the pattern of Jerry Sargeant.

We are all patterns, life is patterns, the entire Universe is made of patterns and we call all of these patterns different things. Take a rock, for example, or a wooden chair. They are both solid and when we sit on them, we sit on them, on top of them, we don't fall through. These objects are also living matter, just like you and I. The energy is concentrated in a small space and this makes the object very hard, and thus stops us falling through. Both of these objects are alive, with the creative force that makes up the entire Universe, bubbling inside of them. They are just less developed in terms of the evolutionary process.

So there is never an in here and an out there; we are at one with the entire Universe. We all live in total harmony and are perfect as we are all part of a much bigger picture, a total reality that is one gigantic, living and breathing organism. When we die we do not die. Our bodies simply decay and our souls move on. They blend back into the formless substance, going back to the spirit world, ready to continue their journey. The essence that makes us up cannot die. We are eternal beings of light, in constant movement, through form and out of form as we too are this beautiful, intelligent energy source.

Now as a part of this vast expansive world, Universe or galaxy we become free. We are born free and should remain free. It's only the voice in our head, our ego, that engulfs our minds with a chaotic view of life and gives a false identity we call our personality. Are you a victim of the world or are you a part of the world?

Well you now know the answer to that. You are the world and the world is you. All the stars, the sun, moon, the sea and every other element is a part of you and you are a part of it. You can only become a victim, living in a false reality, if you choose not to look internally and discover the true identity of you. The real you that makes up a small part of the whole. You are totally creative and very, very special – we all are – and once you believe this and realise, by looking inside for the answers, you will feel at one with all life and your once false identity can be cast away.

Thank it for the experience and then move on, back to peace, love and harmony.

Harness the Ego

There is no coming into consciousness without pain.

– Carl Jung

For one to truly move forward in their lives, they must harness the ego. This takes dedication and practice and a relentless will to want to perfect you as a human being and reach your optimum, in terms of love, happiness and energy. The only way to do this is to see the truth in who and what you really are.

For many human beings, life is like a living hell because they are trapped in their minds, with their best friend, Mr Ego. Mr Ego is a bully and if you let him he will take control of your life and ensure you live a life ruled by fear, anger, frustration, hatred and, to be perfectly honest, keep you in a dysfunctional state of being. Our mind builds up conceptual appearances of other humans, circumstances and events and everything has a label and a judgement is passed, without knowing the truth or evaluating the situation. The mind hangs, draws and quarters its victims without a second look.

The ego likes it this way; it has a purpose and an identity when it's judging others and ridiculing them for the way they look, or even their behaviour. Wars are created because Mr Ego likes conflict. When conflict is in the air Mr Ego feels comfortable and has a sense of strength, even though this strength is temporary and will pass and another battle or war will need to be created to feed the hunger of this troublesome child.

We can, however, harness the ego and take back control of our minds. To do this we must understand the truth. The truth is that we are all special – you know that already, but just in case you had forgotten I thought I would remind you again. The power that lies within you is extraordinary, infinite. You just need to be aware that it's there and be willing and open minded to take a peek.

Once you do you will not look back. The sense of perfection when you connect with this expansive, ever living, never ending force, is immaculate. That's the only way I can describe it. The sense of stillness and total aliveness is there; you are it. You are this force and once you realise it exists and experience the sense of total light energy that is the essence of you, your life will change forever.

To bring you into you and connect, you just have to come into this place from time to time. Take a few deep breaths. As you do you must empty your mind and come into your body, your heart space. When you bring yourself into your body you will feel the awareness and stillness that I am talking about. You will feel alive and feel love for everything around you, maybe for the very first time.

Do this regularly throughout the day. The more you do it the more you will remain in this place. Your ego will always try and butt into your quiet time with distracting thoughts. All you need to do is acknowledge it, and then bring yourself back on track and back into the space of light and harmony, where you are at one with the Universe. To do this focus on your breath. Breathe deeply. In through your nose, right down to the pit of your stomach and back out again very slowly. Feel your mind empty and then a lightness fill your being.

The ego thrives in two ways and if you are aware of them both it's easier to deal with. The ego sees other human beings as either enemies, or stepping stones. An enemy to create conflict with or a stepping stone to enable you to advance in life. There is no goodness in either. You see, Mr Ego is always looking for what's next, viewing the future with envious eyes, wanting to create more and have more of everything, but it is never satisfied. You and I both know it will never be satisfied as long as it's looking externally for the answers, to the future to better its current situation, or to the past for excuses and blame as to why it's not feeling fulfilled.

If Mr Ego is not looking on with envious eyes the attention of its focus may be worry. Thoughts may infiltrate your mind of futuristic events that may never take place and probably won't. As human beings we worry about trivial matters such as not being able to afford the phone bill or what if I get to this meeting and it doesn't go to plan. If Mr Ego had his way you would be sent down the river without a paddle to float helplessly on your journey, forever worrying about what may or may never happen. By being still, living right here in the now, in the present moment, you strip the ego of its power and take control of your life.

When a negative thought, which could be one full of judgement towards another or the fear of the future, enters your mind space, do not let it pull you in. It will be like a magnet or hunting dog chasing the scent of a fox into the woods. It will suck you into a world of misery inside your head. All of which does not really exist of course. It is an illusion. Mr Ego can also be very tricky. He may start off with a thought of something completely irrelevant and as soon as you latch on to this thought, one thought will lead to another and before you know it you are standing on a bridge in the mental realm, about to jump off because life is so torturous.

Don't let him fool you. Be aware at all times and ensure that the thoughts in your head are thoughts that you have intentionally put there through focused thought, on what it is that you want to think about. After all, if used correctly your mind can help you manifest anything that you would like to experience here on Mother Earth.

Clear your mind, come into your heart space and from here clarity will be born. This clarity offers a blank canvas to create the magic you want in your life through concentrated and focused thought. That of your own design.

Love created you, the entire Universe. Let the sun within you shine bright and burn through any dark clouds that are obscuring your vision.

Enter the Presence

Love created you, the entire Universe. Let the sun within you shine bright and burn through any dark clouds that are obscuring your vision.

– Jerry Sargeant

We are at one with all things, all creatures, great and small. There is no inside and no outside. There is not you and the outside world. The outside world is not an object or an artefact. Just as you're not an object or an artefact. Both are living and both are one of the same. We view ourselves as mechanical in the western world. If you look at a picture in a book on biology in school, one that describes the human body and its functions, you will see food entering the mouth, going down the throat and through a whole system, a mechanical system, until the food is digested and the nutrients are transported around the body, and the rest comes out the other end.

If something goes wrong with our bodies, for example, we become ill or have some sort of disease, we go to the hospital. Again this is a system and the doctors in the hospital treat us like a mechanic services a car. But you know, all ailments can be fixed from within, we don't need doctors and hospitals for diseases. After arriving at the hospital, we are asked to put on a blue gown and are stuck in a wheelchair, even if we can walk. We then go through a range of different specialists, who deal with their particular part of the body, and none can deal with each other's areas as they just specialise in their own area which could be the heart, brain, eyes, ears or spine and so on.

After careful examination, we are given drugs and/or are operated on. The majority of human beings are not seen as nature, as natural beings, at one with all elements that make up the entire Universe. We are seen as mechanical people who have to be serviced and so the thought of this deeper presence within each and every one of us is foreign. How could this possibly be?

Within us all lies this immense power that I have mentioned in this book. I have said that you are incredible, powerful beyond belief, and this is so true. You, as a human being, have the capabilities to do anything you want to do in your life, regardless of what it is.

To enable each and every one of us to reach our true potential, we have to connect with the power that fuels us. Inside us all is a being of light. You are a being of light, as I am. We all are. Over the years our light has been dampened out by negative thought patterns but one thing is sure: this light never goes out. The inner spark is always burning, deep within us.

If you take a deep breath right now and focus on that breath... Let it go in and out very slowly. Take another and keep going, and as you do, feel yourself come out of your mind and into your body or your heart space. As you do this you will become aware of a sense of stillness. When you are in this moment you are connected with source, with the essence of you, the being that you truly are. Here you should feel peace as you focus on your breath and nothing else. This is the stillness, the peace and tranquillity that we need to bring back into our lives. Awareness and ego cannot coexist. Awareness dissolves the ego.

Try sitting there in stillness and focus your attention on your hands. Focus on the energy in your hands. Breathe deeply and slowly and focus on that energy. You will feel something deeper, something beyond your hands. This energy will grow and expand and feel larger than your hands. Why is this? It's because you are energy and energy cannot be contained within your physical body. Your energy is the entire Universe and can fill this world. This is the incredible power you are. Your entire being is special. You have the power to live in harmony, be happy always and live always with love and compassion.

When you are in this state, you are present, in the moment, and nothing else matters. Here and now you are connected with the Universe, the energy that created you and me and every other living thing on this planet. The trees, animals, plants, flowers and every object you can possibly see. Everything around you right now, the table, chairs, walls, whatever you can see, is alive. Also the space between everything is not just space. Space is just as alive as you are. Without the space you would not be.

If you put your arm and a table under a high powered microscope all you would see is millions of tiny atoms and molecules and lots of space. This is the same for everything else that exists. We are all made out of the same stuff. This formless substance that is alive and thinks. It has a mind. It's invisible but more powerful than you can imagine. This formless substance is the Universe in all its glory. You and I and every other living thing, object or creation is a manifestation of the Universe, living its life through us all, experiencing life in many different forms.

Forms die but the living energy inside each and every form lives on. The soul in our body never dies. You have been around for millennia and will continue to travel to new realms and places of learning and maybe, once again manifest, or maybe not, in human form. You may stay formless for all of eternity, who knows?

One thing I know for sure is that once you rekindle the love from within, your life will change forever. You will become fearless. You will no longer yearn for any material object to satisfy your needs and wants. Jealousy will be abolished from your being. It's not to say that you cannot live a full and meaningful life, one filled with enjoyable objects, such as luxurious houses, dream cars, the man or woman of your dreams or a perfectly healthy body. You must, however, create those things because you want the experiences, and don't forget, as a human being, you deserve those experiences. Being spiritual does not mean you deny yourself the goodness that this planet has to offer. After all you are a spiritual being having a human experience so why not enjoy every human experience that's on offer? Remember, do it for the experience and not because you think it will make you happy.

It's your birthright to live a maximum life. It's your birthright to become successful but first find the inner you, wake up, become aware and find love and peace on earth, inside yourself, and love every other manifestation on this planet, because you know the truth: all others are you and you are all others. Each and every one of us is made from the Universal substance. The creative force of all nature that resides in all of us. You should feel a deep and profound sense of harmony and love for every other human being on this planet, now that you don't judge or feel jealousy, anger or hatred. You are a being of pure light and now you know the truth. Be here and now and ground yourself in the present moment. Focus on what you can see, feel, hear, smell and taste and do so without labelling any of it. Simply feel it, be it. Be here and be present.

Words can't describe the feelings of joy and emotion that are spilling from my heart right now, as I am writing this. Wow, you really are incredible. I see the smile in your heart and the smile on your face and the light shining even brighter than before. Being present in the moment is the key to unlocking the answers you seek. It's in this stillness the Universe can flow through you with ease. It's in this beautiful tranquil place of Zen that your thoughts disappear and the Universal vibration is allowed to fill your heart with love and peace and direct you on your journey. Coming out of your mind and into your heart space is the answer. Creating this space and living from this place will give you immense clarity on life itself.

Creating space and awareness will enable you to react accordingly
to all situations in life and usually that reaction is no reaction at all,
not in the disempowering sense you will have been used to before.
You can treat any situation, event or other human being with utmost
respect and with a sense of sincere compassion as you know they are
learning or you are being taught. Living in the present moment with
no thoughts of the past of future will enhance your powerful being to
love the life that you are living.

Being present dissolves all worry, stress or any negative thought
patterns which may have recycled themselves throughout your life
up until this point. Creating space will allow your heart and soul to
be free from the torment the mind and your ego can bring upon it.
Never hurry, never be in a rush. Just take your time and you will see
the world around you slow down and go at your pace. On the flip
side it can also suck you in and speed your life up and this is when
you lose control and feel a sense of helplessness. Take your time as
time is no more when you live in the spaciousness of your timeless,
boundless and ever peaceful heart.

Creative Connection

If there is something great in you, it will not appear on your first call.
It will not appear and come to you easily, without any work and effort.

– Ralph Waldo Emerson

Now you know the truth, the truth that your conditioned mind had been covering up all of your life and, maybe, many lives before this one. You are now re-connected to source and this power will be the jewel that ensures the rest of your days on this beautiful planet are paved with glory.

Now that you are reconnected and you understand that all creations, all living forces on this planet, are made up of the same stuff as you are, and are just different forms or manifestations of the Universal substance, living and experiencing all there is to experience, here on Mother Earth, you will feel a strong sense of love for all other human beings, plants, animals, flowers and any other object on this planet. As all objects too are alive.

You will feel love for everything. You will also start to feel more love yourself and start to appreciate all the elements that make up this world. The simplest of tasks will become enjoyable when you are centred in the present moment. I can go for a walk and sit by a tree for hours, feeling it breathe as I breathe with it in unison. We are one of the same after all. If you lie on a rock and close your eyes, you can hear the breeze, feel the rock breathing and feel the connection with the birds and any other animals and/or trees that may be around. If you listen intently, come into your awareness, you will truly feel the vibration of every living cell on the planet.

When you open your eyes, the colours of everything will be enhanced, brighter and full of energy. It's the most amazing experience. The great thing is, it doesn't have to be just an experience. This is how life can be for you, every second of every day, from here on in, as long as you remain centred and in your space, in your peaceful state where you are fully conscious and connected with source, living inside the Universe, breathing in unison with the Universal vibration.

Now as well as feeling the love for all things on Earth there is another element to the equation. When you come into this state you not only connect with the Universe and feel the love for everything, you also find your creative centre. The place from which all things have been and will ever be created.

It's here, when you are aware and conscious, that you can use your mind to create and manifest whatever it is that you want. When you are in this place, you can use the most powerful tool that you possess to your advantage. Your mind when ruled by the ego is your worst enemy and you can become imprisoned in the walls of your mind. Your mind, however, when used correctly and constructively, can produce for you anything and everything that you desire. When you place a thought inside your mind, of something that you want or don't want, it will manifest, every time, without fail.

You mind is like a garden: seeds will always flower – you just have to ensure that you plant those seeds which will help you enjoy life fully. Those seeds that will enable you to experience all there is to experience here on this planet.

Why not plant the seeds that will bring you your perfect partner? Seeds that will take you to your dream destination? Seeds that will bring peace and joy to this planet where every human being is fed, watered and given shelter? Let's use our minds as a collective global group, to bring this world into alignment and give our Mother her health back. She has suffered long enough and we can end her suffering by leading by example. First and foremost we must bring through our own light, and let it radiate twenty four hours a day, seven days a week, without fail. You have the power and so does every other incredible human being on this planet.

It's time to stand up and sing this message from the rooftops, far and wide and shine your light to the deepest darkest parts of the planet. Remember there is light everywhere and when others see your light, theirs will fight hard to shine through. And shine they will, as the light in us all is powerful.

Others just need a spark of hope and some motivation, a sign just like I did. There are messages throughout this book that will have resonated with you – that's why we wrote it, to give you the tools needed for you to re-connect once again.

The kingdom of heaven is within you. This is what Jesus said thousands of years ago. He knew the truth back then. Many others have known the truth since Jesus. He was a pioneer, a being of light, who tried back then to help humanity regain its power. Now there are many like Jesus, who are spreading the word. You may be next. Be strong and fear nothing as now you are standing in your light. You are protected and powerful beyond belief. Use this knowledge and wisdom for the greater good and go forth.

Light up your life and the lives of others around you.

Surrender

*The process of life should be the birth of a soul. This
is the highest alchemy, and this justifies our presence
on Earth. This is our calling and our virtue.*

– Henri Frédéric Amiel

It boils down to two choices; both involve surrender of the soul.
Option number one is that you surrender to the mental mayhem, and
control of the mind, inflicted by your best friend, Mr Ego.

Option number two is that you surrender to the Universe, with faith
and trust, knowing that you are in safe hands, being guided, every
step of the way, to eternal glory.

The latter is the path I have chosen, along with many others who
have stepped forth into the light. The moment you hand yourself
over to God, the Universe, that feeling of space and awareness, that
total connection with your eternal energy source, you will start to
float. Like a man or woman, relaxing on a small boat, lying down in
the summer sun, drifting down the river of life.

Effortlessly, you will drift, left to right, faster and slower, swaying
slightly with the gentle current. As the days pass by and each
moment drifts into the next, you will realise that the past has no
relevance and neither does the future. All that matters is right here,
right now, as the sun beats down on your face and the river of life
keeps unfolding. As you drift round one bend another stretch of river
opens up. Life will keep unfolding naturally, in the most harmonious
way if you just let it be.

All you have to see is the few inches in front of your nose or a few hundred feet down the road. You do not need to worry about what is looming around the corner. Live in trust with a faith so strong and pure, knowing that you are capable of dealing with whatever life throws your way. You are powerful beyond measure and have the skills required to tackle it all.

I was sat there one day and closed my eyes. I said, 'I am ready, do what you want with me. I have learned my lessons and now I know I have a job to do, a duty to fulfil. I am open, and I surrender to you.' I was talking to God, to me, to the Universe, to it, if you can call it an it, that is. Really it is nothing, but everything at the same time. There are no words great enough for what this place or state of consciousness is.

It is what it is, and that is, it just is.

As soon as you stop swimming upstream and fighting against the natural flow of life and in turn the Universe, your life will become easy. No longer will you struggle on the treadmill of life. It's time to relinquish control and stop fighting with something that is so strong and so powerful that you have no control over it anyway. It will do what it wants with you. Like a man or woman in a stormy sea, the power of water becomes so apparent that often he or she will surrender and stop fighting for survival.

I am not suggesting that you should give up but merely go with the natural flow. Step inside your creative centre and let it guide you. Let it show you through thoughts, feelings or emotions. Let it show you the way. Let it guide you in the best possible fashion. In a way that resonates and suits you as a human being. If you are open it will find a way of connecting with you.

Invite it into your life just as you would a stranger, in off the streets, who was suffering from lack of food and shelter in snowy conditions. You would open your door to a stranger – you would not let them reside in the snow, to meet possible death through cold and hunger. Your compassionate side would take over and you would do what felt right.

Invite the space into your life. Day by day, keep inviting it in, and eventually like the stranger on your door step, you will have a new best friend. And soon the tables will turn and this best friend will find a job and become successful and then give back love and affection to you, for the good deed you did that day, by saving his or her life from the cold and hunger.

The Universe, once you invite it into your life, will consume your entire being, your mind, body and soul again, and eventually, it will be like your new found mother. Caring for you, like its new born child. Feeding, clothing, sheltering, guiding and nurturing you with so much love and eternal affection, that you could not face life without this new found joy and peace, ever again.

Meditation

How many people are trapped in their everyday habits;
part numb, part frightened, part indifferent? To have a
better life we must keep choosing how we are living.

– Albert Einstein

We have discussed in brief that meditation is a useful way of connecting with spirit and your internal, creative energy source. I want to give you more of an insight into meditation and some useful pointers to guide you on your inward journey.

Meditation is a chance to connect with reality as when you're being still the essence of who and what you truly are rises to the surface in the space that you create. The illusionary reality we believe as being real is put on hold as you travel inward to harness a state of love and compassion.

Meditation should not be performed to achieve anything. It is paramount that you understand that meditation is a quietening of the mind. A time for you to shut down, shut up and relax your entire being. Forget about the outside world – it will still be there when you stop meditating and step back in to it. It will still be there hours, days or even weeks and years later. Time is irrelevant. Do not think of a time. Let yourself go and fully submerge into the moment.

You can sit up – crossed legged, in the lotus position works well. There is no standard method that is right. Do what feels right for you. It is important to be grounded though and these positions do offer you a grounded position. I sometimes meditate lying or sitting in bed or in a comfy chair with my feet flat on the ground. Meditating in nature, for me works best. You should experiment and not be rigid in your approach.

You should sit still and focus on your breath. To start off with, do it in a place where you will not be bothered. After enough practice you could meditate in the middle of Times Square, and not be disturbed but for now find a quiet environment.

Start by breathing in and out as slowly as possible. Focus on your breath. Breathe in through your nose and out through your mouth. Really bring your concentration onto your breath, and keep it there. The more you focus the more you will notice yourself not thinking. You will feel yourself coming into your body and out of your mind. This is what you want: perfect.

As you do your ego may kick in and say something like 'hasn't this gone on long enough?' Or 'come on this is boring and a waste of time'. Just acknowledge the voice and come back to your breathing. Don't try and fight anything, relax at all times and let it flow. Nothing is right or wrong in this situation; it is just what it is and it is perfect.

As you come further into your body you will feel a certain aliveness within you and you will feel your body's natural energy field all around you. You will also see the light that is you, the light that is within you. You will feel a sense of love for yourself, maybe for the very first time because for the very first time you realise, see and feel that you are a timeless being of light, so beautiful and are at one with all creation.

You may feel a sense of love for everything around you for the very first time, as you realise that you, all others and all things are at peace and are one eternal living energy field, connected at source, by love and light.

As you continue to breathe you will notice the breaths are getting longer and slower and that is perfect. This means you are coming into yourself even more. Just breathe and float and stay perfectly happy and relaxed, acknowledging any thoughts and then once again letting them go. You may feel and hear noises such as birds or traffic outside, again just acknowledge these feelings and thoughts, feel at one with them and come back to your breathing.

Meditation should never feel like a chore. It should be exciting, and you should never feel that you have no time for it and so sacrifice it for work, or another conceptual activity in the illusionary world. The best work you can do is this, meditating and enjoying your own company and the presence within you and the oneness of all creations and manifestations of you, here on this beautiful planet.

When the time is right to stop you will know. Stop when it feels right. You may find your legs getting uncomfortable. If they do that's fine. Stop and come back to it tomorrow. The more you do it, the easier and more naturally it will flow. If you have an office job or work in an environment that is fast paced, an option would be for you to step out of this world and meditate, even for a few moments, several times during the day. It will actually make you a more productive human being and your performance levels will go through the roof.

If you work at a computer or on a phone all day, stop, and for thirty seconds to a minute, close your eyes and focus on your breathing. Meditate and take your attention completely off what you were doing. It is in this place, remember, that you also connect with your internal creative centre and this is where new ideas, knowledge and wisdom originates from. If you are in a high-powered job where you constantly have to meet targets and agendas then this activity, several times throughout the day, will be more beneficial to your chances of success and inevitably your results.

I have used meditation in companies that I either ran or assisted with in their performance and it works a treat. Healthy eating, exercise and meditation are proven methods of accelerating the performance of any company. I have seen it with my own eyes, many times.

If you are a business owner I would encourage you to offer your staff a period of up to fifteen minutes per day, on top of their designated lunch or coffee breaks, to relax their minds. I guarantee you will be thanking me.

You can use other tools to assist you with your meditation such as gongs, bells or crystal bowls. The sounds made by these instruments really bring you into the presence. That sound you hear when a gong rings is the presence through and through in all its glory. That delayed sound that carries on humming is the expansive awareness within you in all its glory, sending feelings of inner peace straight through your soul.

I used to visit a man whose name is The Crystal Child. He lives in New Zealand and his home is like a crystal cavern, from across the globe. The feeling of energy in his house is overpowering. Often you feel nauseous when not used to it and often dizzy. It's mind blowing. The Crystal Child performs crystal bowl meditations and if you ever get the chance I highly recommend one. The different size bowls give off different sounds that connect with the different chakras, on your body.

The state of consciousness you enter into is... I do not have words for it. It is complete consciousness. The feeling we should all be feeling, every second of every minute, a sense of aliveness that gives us super powers. It is nothing and everything at the same time. It is you and I. It is creatures great and small. Every manifestation is the Universe playing a different game, having fun, experiencing life in a multitude of magnificent ways.

Group meditations are also powerful. A group of human beings, all in that place of Zen at the same moment gives off a powerful flow of healing energy to the world. This is why the faster we spread the word, the better. The more of us that meditate the quicker the world will find truth and wake up and the awareness of the entire planet will be at one once more.

Love is the key. Stillness will create the space for love to disseminate throughout our new world. A new dawn is approaching on this planet. By you raising your own internal vibration you are raising the vibration and enhancing the frequency across life's system of intricacy. It's beautiful. You are the creator. Start creating and enjoying this wonderful time and space. Love you. Love the world. Love life and be all that you can be.

Visualisation

When you are inspired by some great purpose, some extraordinary project, all your thoughts break their bonds; your mind transcends limitations, your consciousness expands in every direction and you find yourself in a new, great and wonderful world. Dormant forces, faculties and talents become alive, and you discover yourself to be a greater person by far than you ever dreamed yourself to be.

– Patanjali

Meditation and visualisation are similar but very different. As previously discussed, meditation is an exercise which allows you to connect with source, with love, with light, your internal energy source.

Visualisation is where you can live out what you want your life to be like in your mind and as you do so you will connect and send out these pictures and, by the law of attraction, what you want will be brought to you. You must never see the images as a future representation of your life. You must see it as now, as if it's already a reality. If you see it in the future, it will always remain in the future. The only time and space that exists is the present. Everything else is illusory.

The past has happened and the future will happen but when you arrive there or go back there, if it's regression, you will at that time be in the present. So really all there is is now, the present moment. So when you visualise you must see the life you want as the life you already have. Then the Universe can move events, circumstances and fellow humans to make your dreams a reality. Other human beings will become unconscious agents of the Universe, working with you for the greater good of humanity.

Before this can happen you need to ensure that you are acting, and by acting I mean visualising, from the right place. This place is your creative centre, where all possibilities lie. To commence visualisation, you must at first, meditate to bring yourself into your space of awareness. Once there you can ask yourself, what is it that I am supposed to be doing? What is my life mission? What is my true purpose?

Once you ask the question, you may get a visual answer, in the form of an image in your mind or you may hear verbal communication – either way you will instinctively know what you are supposed to be doing. So many people just decide that a certain project or dream is what they should be doing. The reason they think it is, is due to the thought processes of the rational thinking mind. This sometimes works and embarking on these ventures can be relatively successful.

There is a big however, though. Why swim upstream when you can swim downstream? If you go inside yourself and ask the oneness, the divine energy source that created you, that is you, the answers will be from source, and the path is that of the one you chose when you were sitting on your cloud. If you act from the rational thinking mind's suggestions, the one ruled by the ego, you can find yourself working very hard, when really, it should just flow and be easy.

When you follow the guidance from spirit, you will embark on a mission that is so perfect, you do not even have to try. You will have to take action, however, because without action nothing would happen, but you will not have to try and force the issue. You can just relax, knowing what the end result is and be ready to act when an opportunity arises.

When you act you will be acting with faith because your intentions are pure; they are derived from pure thought and from the living intelligence that created this world and knows what you should be doing. It's only the ego that makes you think you should be doing things you shouldn't and you get the ideas from external third party information and images you see in your daily lives.

Visualise from your creative centre and choose the perfect path – it's already been mapped out for you and the path has been created by the great mind of the one, of God itself. If you knew that you could have an enjoyable, relaxing ride, as you journey through your life knowing that everything was going to turn out well – would you not follow it? Of course you would! Well now you know and can trust in the Universe to guide you and let you live your life, instead of struggling and fighting for survival in the crazy, illusionary world of our ego fuelled mind.

Daily meditation is crucial. The more regularly you undertake this practice the better. I would recommend visualisation at least once a day. The more you practise these techniques the easier it will become and you will find your own perfect order and what works for you. Do not put pressure on yourself. It should feel natural and easy. Do not aim for certain periods of time; do what feels right and as you do more of it, you will instinctively know.

Have fun with it and relax with it. Let your mind flow. Don't try and control it too much. Don't put up barriers. Let your mind be free to wander and explore and dream how it wants to dream.

Your mind is so powerful. Start using it constructively to enhance your own life and the planet itself. Your time on this earth, in this human body, is a small blip in the vast ocean of time. Make every second count. Make every heartbeat mean something. Live your life with maximum energy and let the genius within you shine bright, elevate this world and create a legacy for others to follow and be inspired by. You really are the inspiration that this world needs. God didn't create you to play small. You were created to live at a level of world class, a level of extraordinary. Raise the bar, crush your fears and grow into a mountain of power.

Education

*In order to awaken your greatest life, it's important
that you die while you are alive.*

– Unknown

When we are born, out of this world, parents should be saying to
their children, welcome to the world. It's a crazy place with lots of
rules and here are the rules that will allow you to play the game of
life as best you can. Then hopefully, when you grow up, you can make
some better rules, and make the world a better place.

Instead we say to our children: welcome to the world, you are lucky
to be here. You are not good enough as you are and there are many
lessons to be learned. You're actually quite a mess so we are going
to send you to school, where there are teachers, and these teachers
know everything there is, to prepare you for the real world. They will
control you, play with your mind and whip you into shape, and one
day you may resemble a perfect human being.

If only we told our children the truth. If only the educational system
taught our kids the most important reality that there is for anyone
on this planet to understand. This force that lies within us all, is the
essence of the make-up of the entire Universe. This being the case,
why is it not the number one subject in all school systems across the
entire globe?

We should be teaching our children about life instead of filling their
minds with facts and figures. Yes, some of them may have their
place but quite honestly, how relevant are they? Why not teach our
children about relationships, love, how to eat correctly and exercise

properly and why. Let's give our children an insight into meditation and how to relax and focus. We should be encouraging our children to dream and become successful. Let's teach them about gratitude and how important it is. Every child has immense power within them; school should be teaching them how to unlock it, harness it and use this incredible power to create the most amazing lives for themselves. If a child shows an interest in music, that's what they should learn the majority of the time. We should encourage them to pursue what feels natural and energetic for them. There is no one mould fits all; however, that is what we have based our entire educational system on for years.

It's about creation and our children have so much to teach us. My son came home from school and said, 'The teacher wanted us to watch the news in the classroom.' He is eight years old. He got up and walked out, saying, 'I will not watch that – it's too negative.' I am happy my children know the truth and will stand up for what is right. Asking a child to watch the news at school to me is a hideous crime when there are so many amazing subjects about life itself that they could be taught. Our whole educational system needs an overhaul.

I want to give you an example of the system and how it aims to control our children. My daughter came to me with her Maths homework recently and said she couldn't work out the answer. So I showed her a solution. She turned to me and said she had to work it out a different way. She told me that there was one way and one way only and that she would be punished if she didn't do it like that. I couldn't believe what I was hearing.

The next morning we tried to go over it again and my daughter became very upset. I agreed to come into school and speak to her teacher. When I got there I explained the situation and that my daughter was not a robot. She was a creative human being and surely finding a solution was the answer. The conversation was in-depth and the teacher turned to me and said, 'I totally agree with you, Jerry. The government has brought out new rules and regulations this year and even if the children get the right answer they will be marked wrong if they don't work it out a certain way.' How crazy is this concept? We are breeding robots not human beings.

I want to tell you another short story. One that shocked me. My godson who is six years old goes to a private school in Cheltenham, England. His mother took him into school the other day and spoke to his headmaster regarding his development. The headmaster turned to his mother during the conversation and said the following: 'My job, Mrs Franz, is to take children through the educational system in such a way that when they leave school they work in the £60,000-£90,000 a year wage bracket and conform to society's rules and regulations.'

What is even more ridiculous in my eyes is that the government wants to fine the parents for not sending their children to school. So in other words we have to send our kids in to be brainwashed and turned into robotic government-conforming androids that pay their taxes, have a low expectation of life and live in a bubble making the rich richer and living a life which is non-creative and certainly not fulfilling.

All you parents out there, please listen to your hearts. If school doesn't feel right then find an alternative solution or at least educate your children on the system and encourage their freedom and creative abilities. Nurture them and help them grow into the wonderful human beings they are destined to become.

At school we are taught, quite honestly, a number of topics that have no real benefit and that add no real value to life itself. At school the nature of who and what we are is stuffed into a dark, deep hole and covered up with concrete, layers upon layers of useless, mind-numbing material that detracts us human beings from our internal source of awareness. As children we enter this bodily realm, with an understanding and awareness of our natural and hereditary power.

The issue is that systems, corporations and governments have enforced controlling measures to dampen our spirits as youngsters, and make us believe that we need to conform, listen and obey and have bred most of humanity in a way in which it will benefit those chosen few. The world's so-called controlling forces have tried to take away the ability for us all to create, by making us think that there is a certain way of living and behaving and that we have no creative ability to go out into the world and create our own life.

We are kept in the educational system as long as possible so that we can accept as much brainwashing as possible. The longer we remain in there the less creative we believe we are and the more dependent we become on the so-called system that is there to serve us and ensure our safety and prosperity. I have to argue, whose prosperity? Are we not lining the pockets of the chosen few by relinquishing our God-given right, our God-given power to create, manifest and enjoy life and experience all there is to experience on this beautiful planet?

As we get older we start to watch the news, listen to the radio and become engrossed in certain TV channels, that feed doubt into our minds, and furthermore condition us to the inevitable outcome that we are slaves and servants to the rich and unholy.

We need to re-design the education system and give our children and our children's children the power to do whatever it was they were sent to Mother Earth to do. We do not have to suffer and accept this way of life. This life where we work for others, to line their pockets and carry with us an almighty burden. That burden of the cover up. The cover up of the truth that lies within, decorated with this illusionary world of war, hunger, illness and poverty.

This illusion is coming to an end. As we spread the message and the world wakes up and smells the coffee, that unforgiving aroma, spiralling up the staircase early in the morning. The smell that carries with it the underlying truth, the essence in all things, the aliveness that resides within each and every human being, here on Planet Earth.

Our children are sacred and we must protect them, love and care for them and ensure they never lose sight of their potential. We must encourage them to believe and stimulate their faith and when they come into our bedrooms at night, saying they are having nightmares or a bad dream, we should encourage this aspect of their make-up. Don't tell them it was a bad dream and that dreams don't exist. Let them know that they are special and ask them to talk about their dream with you and together you can piece together the real life jigsaw puzzle and give them a real answer. An answer, a message that is contained in the dream-like state of consciousness.

I learnt nothing at school that I utilise today in this world I live in. Every experience and life encounter has taught me sufficiently. We should encourage children to get out into the world and try new things. Experiment with ideas. It doesn't have to make sense, it just has to feel right. My whole life has been about feeling my way through, and so may have yours.

Most great leaders, avatars, spiritual warriors, CEOs of companies, have created their lives outside of the educational system. Most successful men and women became so by attending the school of life. It's on this glorious playing field that limitations are no more and boundaries are an aspect of the past. It's here that young adults will run wild, engulfed in their creative centre, protected by their divine energy source and it's here their lives will flourish and one by one each and every soul will become enlightened. They will then rise up, stand tall and be proud as they know who they truly are.

They have learned the most important lesson there is to learn, quite possibly the only lesson that really matters, because, from here on in, once the creative centre is reunited with the aspect of you in this dimension, your life will unfold and no longer will you have to try and force any issues.

No longer will you have to swim upstream, because the magical flow of the Universe will have you lying on an inflatable bed, drifting down the calm and content river of life, floating towards your destiny, allowing you to be happy and relish every second of every day, and every moment here in this magical land.

Mind, Body and Soul

A sound mind in a sound body is a short but full
description of a happy state in this world.

– **John Locke,** *seventeenth-century English philosopher*

Re-connecting to your complete energy source, your spirit, should
be at the top of everyone's list of things to do. Being still makes it
possible. On the other hand, becoming more active will also stimulate
your mind and in turn your body. Becoming a fitter you will keep you
in a more relaxed state in between exercise. You will be calmer and
more focused, making it easier to connect to source. Doing it without
exercise will work; however, it's going to enhance the process.

I have seen many unhappy people in my time become happy. I have
seen many unsuccessful people become successful. I have seen the
most unconfident become the most confident, and the catalyst has
been a little exercise. A little exercise can change your whole mind-
set. It can establish a side of you that you never knew existed.

Exercise releases endorphins that make you happy. Exercise makes
the blood pump and the oxygen flow around the body. Exercise
gets rid of stiffness and gives you more energy. Exercise, full stop,
if performed correctly, will stimulate the body in a way you cannot
imagine until you have come from a life of no exercise to a life that is
fuelled by it.

You mind, body and soul will elevate to levels far beyond your
expectations.

Why do so many of us not exercise?

Maybe you are scared of the initial pain on the road to fitness? Maybe you think you have not got enough time? Maybe you think you can't do it? Maybe you think you can't afford a gym membership? Maybe all your friends like to go out drinking and so you would feel like the odd one out?

I could go on all day, and let this list consume your mind but you get the point. My wife and I run a health and fitness centre, and I have heard all the excuses imaginable. And that's all they are – excuses. You could call some of them reasons due to lack of knowledge. For example, it will hurt too much. If you go from doing nothing to intense circuit training, you probably will. If you made it round without collapsing, you will not be able to walk for a week. It's important to build up the intensity gradually. If you have never done anything previously, start with a ten-minute walk once a day and increase by ten minutes a week for six weeks. At the end of the sixth week, you will be walking for an hour.

You can then start jogging for thirty seconds of every five minutes. That will be six minutes in the total hour. After a week, you can go to one minute of every five minutes. Then out of every one hour, you are jogging for twelve minutes. You can see how it works. It's simple and is manageable.

At our gym, we have beginner's circuits which anyone can do and then advanced circuit training, and other classes in-between that accommodate all levels of ability. Whatever your current state of health and fitness is, start doing something now.

You don't have to join a gym either as there are so many body weight exercises you can do and make routines with. Just start off simple, whatever you can do. Start today and I guarantee you will be thanking me. Exercise is important.

I will leave you with a following, small but important, list of some of the benefits you will receive in return for exercising:

1. Improved moods

2. Increased sex drive

3. Less body fat

4. Increase in energy and focus

5. Stronger bones

6. Stronger muscles

7. Better sleep

8. Increased relaxation

9. Better immune system

10. Lower heart rate

11. Better complexion

12. Weight loss

Why would you not want to exercise? If these are some of the benefits, then you should be allotting time to start exercising regularly. You have already decided you want a better life and that you want to discover the power that lies within you. That's why you're reading this book, right? So make it even better by optimising your general health and well-being through exercising.

Why Nutrition?

Tell me what you eat, and I will tell you what you are.

– Anthelme Brillat-Savarin, *eighteenth-century French writer and epicure*

Developing your mind and the tools and strategies to enhance your life is one part of the puzzle and the other is to give your body and mind the best fuel possible to enhance your capacity to think and play.

Being active will give you so many benefits in life. It will increase your energy levels and focus. It will make your blood pump, your bones healthier, your heart and all the others muscles stronger as well as making you happier and more vibrant about life itself.

Nutrition will enable you, through putting the best fuel into your body, to think more clearly about life and become more focused and in turn allowing you to put to use all the other tools you are learning more efficiently.

Think about this for a second. An incident happens in your life that you need to find a solution for. You must remain cool, calm and collected to handle the situation productively. To do this you need to be in good space. If you are pumping chemicals into your body that distort your mind you may react slowly or ineffectively or maybe negatively and in turn make the situation worse. It's a bit like reacting without breathing – it's never good.

In meat, dairy, fish, processed foods and sugary foods there are chemicals that do not serve us. I for one do not eat meat, fish or dairy or anything processed. The amount of hormones and other chemicals used to enhance the growth of animals is scary. Even organically produced meat products, in my opinion, should be left alone. Now I don't want to scare you off in this chapter. I know I am making some comments that could make you think this is never going to happen. I love my meat, I love my cheese, I love ice-cream. You may eat all of the above. If you do that's OK for now. What I am going to do is set some goals for you to work towards and gradually, over time, you can implement small lifestyle changes that lead to you becoming healthier, happier and more focused in life.

Remember your mind is so powerful and will be a major driver in you achieving your dreams, and in order for your brain to function at peak levels it needs nourishing. It needs to be kept on an even keel and chemicals will throw it out of sync. Sugar itself is a drug that I would consider as harmful as cocaine. You become addicted to it and it rots your body and mind.

Your body carries your soul, the life force within you. It's time to adopt habitual patterns that make your time in this body more pleasurable. Think about this. If you had to go on a long journey, would you like to do it cramped up in a battered old mini, or would you prefer to sit in a spacious, brand new BMW? It is time that you treated your body like a racing car driver would treat his race car. Put good quality fuel into it to receive optimum results. If you poured beer into a race car it would not get you very far.

The way to get the best out of your body is to eat natural food sources – water-rich content food, such as fruit and vegetables, berries and on top of this a mix of nuts, cage-free organic chicken's eggs, salads, beans, lentils and seeds. This is what will help you function at peak levels. This is what you are aiming for in time. Maybe you eat like this anyway. If you do that is fantastic.

If you don't it's also fantastic because eventually you will do. You don't have to throw everything out of your diet at once but I want you to start making small manageable lifestyle changes now.

In the mornings the best food sources to eat are fruits. They go straight through your system and the fructose in the fruits gives you good energy. They help your brain switch on in the morning and also eating nothing but fruits gives your body a chance to detox. One more thing that is crucial in the morning is to alkaline your body. You have either acid or alkaline in your body and when your body is in an acidic state you do not perform, you become unhealthy and disease can set in. Eating lots of greens is essential to keep the pH levels in your body at a level of alkalinity. Your aim is to keep your pH level at 7.2. You can go to a chemist and buy the little pieces of (litmus) paper you can put under your tongue or urinate on and then measure your levels. You can do this and see what your level is currently.

In the morning three options to get your body alkaline are as follows:

1. Drink water with freshly squeezed lemon juice in it.

2. Drink super greens with water. You can buy super greens from any health shop. I prefer Dr Schulze super greens.

3. Options three is to get a juicer and juice some broccoli, cucumber or anything green into a glass and drink it down as soon as you wake up.

In the evening I always have a glass of greens or water with lemon juice to alkaline my body before going to sleep. Doing this enables you to sleep better and get the most out of the time you are lying in your bed.

You may be thinking already, this is so much to remember. That's

OK. Practice makes perfect. Nutrition is no different. It's about implementing a small change every day and before you know it you will have changed your entire lifestyle around. If you want to live long and watch your grandkids grow up, still being able to function and play with them, then a healthy lifestyle is a must. If you want to build a successful business and enjoy it then a healthy lifestyle is a must. If you want to have the best relationships with your wife or husband and children then being a healthy wife, husband or mum or dad is of the utmost importance.

So alkalising your body is important. What next?

The next thing I want to talk to you about is bread. White bread and some brown breads are terrible. It's like tipping cement down a drainpipe. Your body can't function like this. If you are a bread eater cut it back. Maybe once or twice a week and when you do make sure it's wholegrain bread. If possible have rye bread, or spelt and never eat bread late in the evening. Lunchtime would be ideal.

I want to talk to you about protein. Protein is a big myth. Protein companies earn billions so spend a lot on advertising making you think that you need to consume lots of it to build your muscles. Your body actually adapts to whatever amount of protein you put into it. I am not saying to have none. You do need proteins but don't think that they are the most important part of your diet. Fruits and veg will carry you further and make you stronger than bucketloads of protein, whether it be in the form of shakes or meats.

How much protein should you have? Well this comes down to you. People will tell you that you need 1.2 grams of protein per kg of body weight or 1.6 grams per kg of body weight if you're exercising hard. Personally I believe that we are all different and need to find out through trial and error for ourselves and work out what is best for us as individuals.

Play about and see how you feel. Your body will tell you what to eat. If it craves fruits or eggs or maybe something else it's probably for a reason. If it craves sugar it's because it's used to getting it and now you are depriving your body of it so give it sugars in the form of fruits, rather than a Snickers or a pack of Maltesers.

If you're a parent don't give your kids sugar. It's like giving crack cocaine to a crack head. They will want more and will keep consuming it until they are ill, their teeth have fallen out and they feel depressed. If you are a parent and your kids are used to eating sugary foods I want you to know this. It takes approximately 14 days for kids' taste buds to get to like new foods as long as they try it every day. Start weaning them off sugary foods and replacing them with fruit. Sugar is one of the biggest culprits for illness, disease, obesity and behavioural problems. Sugar rots the body and makes us fat. Really, stay away from sugar.

Now I am not trying to scare you here and if you are used to eating these foods don't think it's the end of the world. Now you are aware you can start making changes. Think of how energised you will feel with your new-found lifestyle and it won't take long before you look back and say to yourself, 'I can't believe I used to go to McDonald's and Burger King so often' and if you do at some point taste those foods after being on a clean diet for a few weeks you will really taste the grease and chemicals in them.

I have seen it with so many clients. I have coached people who had the most horrific nutritional rituals – coke and pizza for breakfast, fish and chips for lunch, steak, eggs and chips for dinner and an array of sugary snacks and drinks throughout the day to spike their moods and feed their addictions. If these people can come from 160kgs, lethargic and unhappy to 80kgs of lean body weight, full of confidence and happy in life, then anyone can.

It's just a mind-set. You have to want to and you have to take massive action, get into the right state of mind and act with certainty. You have to know that if you don't make the lifestyle changes then the long term consequences will be traumatic, lead to unhappiness and eventually death. Really and truthfully that's what's on the cards here. The wrong foods equal a negative outcome. Good, nutritious, healthy foods create a confident, energised human being that will take massive action and go out into the world and make their dreams a reality.

Now you know that fruit should be consumed in the morning after alkalising your body with lemon and water, super greens or juiced greens. You know what type of breads to eat if you must eat bread and how often. You are also now aware of the damage sugary foods and drinks can have on you.

Now let's discuss processed foods, meat and dairy products.

Firstly, anything that comes out of a packet will have some form of chemicals in them or the food itself will be stripped of all its goodness. Filling yourself up with food that contains chemicals or has no nutritional value is senseless. Here's the thing. If you don't know, you don't know. But now I am pointing it out to you another option is on the table.

Fresh foods are the best. Eating them raw is even better. When we cook our vegetables we lose precious nutrients in the process. When we package any foods the nutritional value goes down, and anything processed is a waste of money and time – unless you are looking to end your life earlier that is. If that's your goal then go right ahead.

Now dairy for me is a no-no. Even organic. Milk and cheese clogs up your system and the chemicals used to enhance the growth of animals are extremely unhealthy. A lot of people drink milk for calcium; however, there is enough calcium in a number of green vegetables. You just have to decide whether or not you want a healthy, well-oiled machine that functions at peak levels to transport your soul and control your life or not.

For me my body is my temple. It should be the same for you. Care for it and nurture it and give it the best fuel possible so it can give back to you in terms of energy and enthusiasm. You are what you eat. It's so true.

Now meat products is the next subject of discussion and I will tell you why leaving them out of your body is the better option. We have a system in our bodies called the lymphatic system. It's controlled by your breathing. This system is responsible for taking away all the dead blood proteins and excess waste that your cells don't need and excrete. As you breathe it takes these toxic chemicals out of your body. Animals function the same. When an animal dies it stops breathing and the lymphatic system stops working so all that toxic waste floods through the cell walls and into the muscles and stays there ready for us to consume when we eat our chicken, beef, turkey, pork, fish and so on.

As well as these natural chemicals produced by the body there is all the growth hormones injected into the animal to make it grow faster so that it can be killed and sold quicker to keep up with demand from our growing population and to see faster profits for the farming and dairy corporations. It's big business and unfortunately for you your health is not the primary concern of the men and women that own these companies. Money is their motivator and if they bring you long term pain they are either unaware or simply don't care and turn a blind eye. Or maybe they do care but their love of power and profit is greater than the pain caused to a third person or group of people they will never know.

Now all I am doing here is making you aware of what is best for you. I want you to have the best life possible. I want you to live and experience life in an incredible fashion. I want you to feel twenty when you are 80 – and believe me, that's possible. If you follow these methods you will add many quality years to your life.

Now the most daunting part of this is what do I eat now I can't eat dairy, meat, fish, processed foods, fast foods, sweets, cakes, chocolates etc. Don't worry, there are thousands of easy-to-follow recipes to use.

Before we go on to what you can eat and when, I want to cover fat quickly. There are certain fats such as saturated fats that you don't want to eat and good fats that you do want to eat such as the type of fat found in nuts or avocados. Eating good fat will help you burn the excess fat you may be carrying on your body. Try and have a few nuts or some avocado with every meal.

Now this is not a cooking lesson so a bit of further research on your part will be needed. It's going to be easy. On the internet there are thousands of recipes, tasty nutritious ones, that you can follow.

During this next week I want you to find three breakfast options, three lunch options and three dinner options that you like. Write them down and try them out. This will get you started in the right direction. Remember, Rome wasn't built in a day. Try and implement small changes and work your way up. Maybe you can start by just eating a healthy breakfast and add lunch and dinner in a week or two later, no pressure. Do what feels right.

Now one more thing on nutrition. Get used to grazing. Eat small and often throughout the day. Don't overindulge. As soon as you feel that your body is filling up, stop. If there is food on your plate, leave it. Be proud that you left food and don't feel guilty. Growing up as children our parents pushed us to clean up our plates and conditioned us to believe we should eat everything in sight. This mentality leads to obesity. Eat little and often and as you do your stomach sack will shrink and then less will fill you up. This will help you lose weight rapidly. Never starve yourself. If you're hungry, eat. Even 10 times a day but as soon as you feel full, stop. That's the key.

Respect your body and fuel it with love and natural goodness that will nourish it and give you the best body possible.

In Nature

Our prime purpose in this life is to help others; and
if you can't help them don't hurt them.

– His Holiness the Dalai Lama

Exercising is going to enhance the process and make it easier for
you all round. As well as a little physical exercise entering your daily
regime, why not spend a little time back with nature? Better still, why
not try a little exercise in a natural environment?

Now we are talking. It's one thing exercising and another being in
nature, but to mix the two together is a completely different ball
game and it also maximises your time effectively. Not that we need
to worry about time – after all, it only exists in this realm to help
us get along. Time is really an illusion, a mental thought that is not
necessary once you become fully aware and alive in your conscious
awareness.

Being in nature is beautiful. Just walking along in the fields or woods,
with your new sense of awareness, you can smell all the amazing
smells and look at the dazzling colours of bushes, trees and flowers.
Your new heightened awareness and connection to source will make
everything more prominent. The smell of the bark on an old oak tree.
The smell of the flowers and dew on the morning grass. You will see
nature in a whole different light.

Being in nature is much more effective than being inside a man-
made, manufactured environment. Nature is alive and everything in
nature has a soul, each flower, tree or bush has an energy field and a
being inside that you can communicate with. Being in nature will also

give you the opportunity to communicate with the fairy realm, which is something I do very often.

I often go to a favourite place of mine in Gloucestershire, England. It's a place called Crickley Hill. You can drive up to the lookout point, park your car and walk along through the woods and across the fields looking out over the town.

I often walk right to the very end and there is a small ledge of grass next to some bushes that I sit on. I will meditate for a while, centre myself and then lie down in the grass looking up at the sky. Some days the most amazing things happen to me up there. It is a place in which I fully connect, in the most amazing way. This natural environment brings together all the elements I need to get a clear view on life and what exists here, on Earth and also what lies beyond this dimension, where the denseness is no more.

Only last week I was lying down, looking up at the sky, and I saw hundreds of fairies flying, dancing and jumping all over the place. Like little silvery wisps, about an inch high. Happy as can be, free from all the uncontrollable thinking that takes place here on our planet. They communicate, often as one, like an army of tiny voices all at once, speaking in unison, offering advice and comforting words and showing their appreciation for what I have been doing to help humanity at this stage of evolutionary growth.

You will find yourself, as you become more aware, that you can't walk past any rubbish on the ground, without picking it up and putting it in the bin. If you walk past it you will hear a voice say, go and pick it up or you will feel this immense pull, as though you are being dragged back to pick it up and perform your duty. I never thought I would hear me say this. What stands out in my mind though, is if I can change, anyone can change.

Get out into nature and enjoy it, have fun in it, and more importantly, take care of it. Mother Earth needs our help and you can start by just being in nature, and shining love and light, letting the trees, plants, animals and flowers know that you love them and that as a part of them, being the Universal substance yourself, you will do everything you can to let others know of this great gift that we all share.

Once we all wake up and understand who we truly are and what lies inside us, and makes up our entire being, life and every living element of life will dance together in harmony, for the very first time in thousands of years. This is happening all around us right now; help you by helping us and let the magic begin.

Crystals

Life does not listen to logic; it goes on its own way,
undisturbed. You have to listen to life; life will not listen
to your logic, it does not bother about your logic.

– Osho

Being in nature is an amazing feeling and the more aware you are,
of your true being that resides inside you, the more you will love the
time you spend there. Nature itself is inspirational; however, there is
a storehouse of wealth, knowledge and wisdom, there on tap, for each
and every one of us human beings on this planet.

These gems come in different shapes, sizes, colours and forms
and have an intelligence just like you and I. As you know by now,
everything in the entire Universe is made from the formless
substance and it thinks likes you and I. There is a part of this
Universe though, that has helped me immensely on my journey and
it took me a while to fully understand, and comprehend the power of
these beings.

Crystals are alive and carry knowledge and wisdom and will work
with you, on a spiritual level, to act as guides on your personal
journey. They will also, if asked, show you the way into other
dimensions and give you direct access to a whole new world that lies
around us. A world that is happening right now, in parallel with our
world.

Crystals can also be the doorway to the past and future. I have used
crystals in many meditations to access past lives and see future
scenarios being played out. I remember once I was taken to the

top of a large hill and I sat there. The hill was in Africa and I was looking out over a village and these people needed my help. I didn't understand at the time what this meant but it was not too long after this happened that I was giving money to a charitable organisation and I helped build schools in Africa.

In terms of the future, this is what I believe. I don't know for sure but from personal experiences and evidence I have collected along the way, I believe this to be true. There are a number of possible outcomes for our lives. They are governed by the choices we make. We have a specific goal and mission that we choose before we incarnate and it is our job to stay on track. Obviously we are tested in this dense, earthly plane and many souls stray off track and have to come back again for a second or maybe third chance. Some maybe more.

We have assistance at every turn but some of us cannot see this as we lose our way in the deep, dark and dense forest and never find our way out. I was lost in the forest but was lucky enough to have guides and earthly assistance to ensure my mission was fulfilled. Some are not so lucky and have to come back down and relive it once more, until they succeed and go to a higher place of learning.

The hill vision in Africa was a clear indicator for me that the future has already happened and that I saw a glimpse of one possible outcome. I am so grateful I chose the path that led me there. Other defining evidence for me is déjà vu. So many times I have been in a situation and said to myself 'I've been here before' and played out what I saw in my dream as clear as day. You will, at some point in your life, probably have experienced the same. How can you go somewhere, or do something and know you have already experienced this act? How is it possible if it has not already happened?

I could put it down to coincidence, maybe once, twice at a push but really when this has happened so many times I can't recall most of them, it leads me to think, with a concrete view, that the future has already taken place.

Crystals allow you access to many different dimensions. I have not really experimented with the future, because I know what the future holds will be perfect. I also do not use crystals anymore to access past lives, unless something pressing comes up and I am told to, by my guides or spirit. I will just use crystals when I meditate and if they take me off to a certain place then I will just go there as I trust the Universe and my crystals and know there is a reason for me going and seeing what I am being shown.

If you have not used crystals before then I recommend giving it a go. Many people will give you their views on crystals and say this crystal does this and that one does that and maybe they are right. For me I just go with the natural flow of the Universe and use crystals that I am guided to.

Not long after I started my journey of self-discovery, a flyer came through our front door that had a local fair advertised. It was an alternative fair where they had tarot readings, healers, aura readers and so on. I knew deep inside I had to go as I felt this burning desire to. When I got there I saw a crystal stall and a lady selling all sorts of crystals.

I went to the stand and looked around. There were beautiful coloured crystals, of all shapes and sizes but there was this one tiny, clear quartz crystal that was pulling me in. It was talking to me and wouldn't let me look at any other crystals. I picked it up and it looked shabby and was brown on one side. It was probably the ugliest crystal on the stall. I remember thinking that to myself. Why would I want to buy this one?

I held it up to the light and looked through it. It had some strange configurations on the inside. These small triangular shapes. The lady looked at me and said, 'That crystal belongs with you.' Yeah right, I thought to myself. You are just trying to sell me something. I remember the price of this tiny, brown looking crystal being £20.00. Most of the larger, shinier ones were less expensive. Why was this? I thought to myself.

Anyway, I bought the crystal and took it to show Trish, from the Tree of Life Centre. She looked at it and said, 'This crystal is full of knowledge.' I said, 'How do you know?' She held it up to the light and showed me the triangular configurations I had seen when I saw it earlier. She said, 'This has much to offer you.' I have kept this crystal by my bedside for years. Everywhere I go it goes. Every meditation it is on my base chakra and it guides me well. It has taken me to many places on this Earth and other dimensions and it answers any questions that I ask it.

Crystals will communicate with you and always give you true and honest advice, help and guidance. Communicating with crystals is much like talking to your guides. You have to empty your mind and listen carefully, and just trust what comes into your head. It will take practice. When you empty your mind and come into your presence it's much easier. At times, the ego may jump back in and obscure the answers and guidance you are being given. It will take practice to discern between the two, but I promise you eventually, with regular practice, you will become a master at it.

The more you come into your presence and communicate with spirit the more you will fine tune your entire system. The more you use your crystals, the clearer your channels will be. The same goes for fairies, angels and tree people. They will guide you much the same if you ask for their help and listen.

The more you practise and the more open you are, the more your awareness will heighten and the faster we can bring about a global awareness, and eventually bring back the old communication and telepathy will once more be the order of the day. Experimenting and practising, being open is great. Encouraging others to do the same, and let them know these gifts are available, to them also, is even greater.

The heights that we can reach and the potential that we have is infinite. There are no boundaries with this work. Let's keep pushing and striving to bring peace back into this world and balance back into this Universe.

One by one, friend by friend, stranger by stranger we will enlighten you all.

Fulfilment

If you wish to experience peace, provide peace for another.

– Tenzin Gyatso

Once you reach this place, this state of being, the awareness that lies inside you and is you, a sense of fulfilment will overcome your entire being. Once in this place you will find joy in everything and everyone.

Other human beings in your life, friends, family and total strangers, up until this point, will have been seen as either stepping stones or enemies. Stepping stones that will have enabled you to go on and find fulfilment somewhere else or enemies that have been sent to launch an attack on your sense of who you are.

You will have derived your sense of who you are by the thoughts flying around inside of your head, created by your good friend Mr Ego. When another human being enters your life your ego sees them as a threat and labels them in a certain way that will make you think this or that about them, and inevitably you will see them as a threat in some way, shape or form. If not a threat then you will think thoughts that will have you working out ways in which you can utilise this other human being, to your best advantage, to add value to your own life.

Both are unhealthy. Now you know the truth and will be feeling this enormous power coming from inside. You now know how to connect with your inner energy source, the essence of you and the source that makes up this entire Universe. Now you know the truth you will have total fulfilment from simply being and feeling you.

You no longer need to find your sense of fulfilment from a loved one, a friend or business partner. You no longer need to venture into the material world to find fulfilment. A car or house or any dreamy travel destination will not be able to fulfil your heart and soul. It will only be a temporary satisfaction.

Now you know the truth, you can revel in spirit in all its glory knowing that it will feed you, clothe you, protect you and make you happier than you ever thought possible. The amazing thing is that this power is you, it's resided in you all this time, waiting for this special moment when you realised it was there and re-connected with the light that blesses the world.

This power is you, it's the room you are in, the waves that splash on the beach, the sun that warms the day and the moon that bathes the world in a shiny coat at night. It is your joy, peace and harmony, it's the glow of warmth in your belly as you sit there and just simply be you, knowing that you are safe and live without fear as you are present in this human form, as an incarnated spiritual being of light, living and experiencing all there is to experience here on Mother Earth.

You are totally satisfied and fulfilled from the minute you wake, until the moment your head hits the pillow and every other moment in between. As you move through time and space without a care in the world, because you are simply being you, and everything you do is perfect. It's perfect for this present moment, in this time and space. Nothing is wrong, only right. You are following the path, your path. Just as I am following mine, living my life as Jerry Sargeant, here right now, passing on these messages to you all so you can sail on this boat with me. I feel this feeling always and soon too will you.

This sense of fulfilment because I know the truth and have been living the truth for some time, feels amazing, beautiful. In fact I have no words for how wonderful this ride is. All I know is I want to bring along as many passengers that can possibly fit in this sailing vessel with me.

If we run out of room we will build another boat and fill that one up too. Until eventually there are millions of sailors, creating boats and filling them up with likeminded passengers and sailing out into the sunset to live in this new world, where we work and play in harmony with one another. This new world where time is now more, just a never ending vastness of immense possibilities.

Let the light shine through and fill you up with goodness. Let it nourish you and guide you as you travel on this journey, in this new and ever being you.

Forgiveness and The Revolution

To forgive is the highest, most beautiful form of love. In return you will receive untold peace and happiness.

– Robert Muller, *former Assistant Secretary-General to the United Nations*

There are many elements of love that will bring civilisation into the new dawn where the light consumes the planet and dissolves darkness is the hardest of hearts. Happiness, compassion, joy and peace are all building blocks that are born from love. Another is forgiveness. This almighty and powerful way of being is natural to the core yet so many human beings find it difficult to forgive. Why is this? It's because the ego is in control and the ego likes conflict. The little voice inside your head doesn't like to give in. It creates resistance wherever possible when the key to moving forward is to forgive.

Think back to a time when you forgave someone. Take a moment. Remember that time now. How did you feel the last time you were strong enough to forgive? It felt incredible. Why is that? It's because forgiveness resembles strength and power. A weak mind will turn and run for the cover of blame and frustration. Forgiveness is love shining at its core, pure light emanating from the depths of your soul, shining out into your life to communicate with the one you are forgiving or have forgiven. In other words you are saying I love you. Because forgiveness can only flow from a loving heart.
Whether you are forgiving a parent, spouse, child, friend or business associate or even a total stranger in the street you will always need to create space. Quite often when an incident occurs that must be forgiven our ego dives in, sword drawn ready to attack. Only an

aware human being, living in the present, that has created space by breathing and coming into their heart can deploy the life healing remedy of forgiveness.

The more we forgive the happier we become. When harbouring old grudges or holding onto emotional baggage we are causing pain in our own mind and body and ultimately this pain will flow out into the world. Honouring emotions is mission critical if you are to live happily ever after, raise your vibration and live freely, detaching yourself from the illusory world you live in. Forgiveness is a passageway or a bridge from the old paradigm into the new. A crossing from the illusory world of form into the reality of energy and flow.

It doesn't matter how much you feel hurt or betrayed by a man or woman or a situation, you must learn to make forgiveness your first port of call. If forgiveness feels hard, create space and from the space you will gain clarity. A quietening of the mind will always allow you the opportunity to see the right way forward. Even if you choose its opposite, to not forgive it will be perfect for now. It just shows you that you have work to do. Your aim is to accept this is where you are currently at right now and the next time an opportunity to forgive enters your life, take it.

You will keep getting opportunities to forgive and the tests will get harder or larger and more intense. So my advice would be to forgive now. Forgive always. Re-discover what's natural. Open your heart and forgive once more. Wars are created because people cannot forgive. An eye for an eye as the old saying goes. This is the ideological way of old. The old world we are leaving behind will continue to live by this code of misplaced honour whilst the children of light with an open heart march bravely into paradise, into the rising of peace.

A world full of laughter and harmonious chatter. A world that will have no hierarchy. A peaceful land stripped of all the non-essentials, brought back to its simplest form. A world with the most powerful currency in the universe, love. What is happening on Mother Earth right now is global consciousness taking place. A coming together of human beings with a common goal. A movement, a huge movement is in full flow. A revolution is in operation because now is the time. It's the time when we, as a global community, are at a crossroads. There are two directions in which we can travel.

One is deep into a denser environment where a lack of light is the controlling factor. There are forces at work that are trying to keep humanity in this place. The other option, however, will be the one I am sure you will choose after reading this book, whereby you follow me and thousands of others into the light, where the vibration is enlightened by the truth. The truth that lies within each and every soul on this planet.

Now you know how special you are and the enormous capabilities you have, and the power that lies within both, your internal and external energy source can provide for you at every turn THE energy and resources needed. It will clothe, feed, shelter, guide and love, unconditionally, each and every human being, animal, plant, flower and every other object on our planet.

This power caused me to wake up and it has caused you also. It will cause every other human being on this planet to do the same and gradually, like a snowball rolling down a hill, picking up speed and gaining in size and strength, will keep on moving. The revolution has started. Just as you and I and many others are in this beautiful space right now. More will come and more will see the truth.

The shackles of the illusionary, greed-fuelled world that has manipulated mankind for centuries are dissolving and the controlling measures that have weighed the human race down are slowly losing their grip. The special forces of love and compassion are growing stronger and brighter by the hour.

You cannot stop this force; it's natural, powerful and full of the love of many minds of men and women across the globe, still in the peace that lies within. Conscious, living in heaven, that special place. The only place that, once you have visited, you will never again want to live outside the kingdom you have now found.

Stand strong in your faith and never let another, unenlightened human being dim your light or quench your faith. Some may try and some may succumb if they are not standing in their truth, at peace with, and connected with the formless substance, the creator of this magical Universe.

Regardless of what temptations you face, from third party sources in life, or no matter how much of an onslaught the egoic mind slams down on you, remember it's not their fault, they are not as enlightened as you are and have not found that natural, special place. Others may try an emotional play on you but remember, it's just emotion, and emotions pass, like the waves coming into shore from the sea.

You are getting stronger and stronger by the minute and your light is shining brighter. Use this light and shine it bright wherever you go. Be fearless and spread the word. Lead by example and show the world how good it feels to live in the present moment, with your mind fixed upon the present moment, feeling the feelings of eternal joy and happiness because you are happy being you. Happy and grateful for all that life has offered you. All the places that life has taken you and all the experiences that you have experienced already and the many more you know are coming.

Live your life with love. It's love that started this wondrous revolution and it's love that will see it through to the end. Do your part and be the love that you are. Love everything and everyone as much as you can with an abundance of love and glorious light.

Paradise

Every day think as you wake up, today I am fortunate to be alive, I have a precious human life, I am not going to waste it.

– His Holiness the Dalai Lama

I believe that every human being on this planet has a finite number of heartbeats and I for one do not intend to waste any of mine.

– Neil Armstrong

I am crying with joy, happiness and delight. We have reached this point. You have come so far and have completed this part of your mission. You were attracted to the book and bought it without hesitation and now you have read it to the end. This is the final chapter; it's all roses and smiles right now.

You are about to live out a real life fairytale. You are in a position to see the light and send the light, to distant lands, far and wide, spreading it across the globe and further afield. You can send this message and focus your light on all walks of life on this planet and the next.

This is where the real work begins. Now is the time for you to live authentically, with love, compassion and in full acceptance. I am not suggesting this will easy, because for many it's very difficult. Know this however; you are vibration, love, light, an infinite, boundless, timeless energy source and the power you possess, is extraordinary. Life will never give you anything you cannot handle. You have the power to face your fears and overcome every challenge.

I want you to start taking the action of a hero. No longer will you accept victimhood. Each day you are breathing the universal oxygen, truly live your life. Get up each morning nice and early. Join me in the 5am club. Exercise for twenty minutes, meditate for twenty minutes and then read a book on philosophy or a book written by a successful man or woman who fulfilled their life mission. Maybe you can read a book on Mother Teresa, JFK, Nelson Mandela, Albert Einstein; as you study others you will gain in knowledge, just as when you study yourself. Start eating like an athlete, loving like a saint and living like an adventurer.

Cristopher Columbus discovered the new world because he took the perpendicular approach. He sailed straight out to sea. He ventured outside of his comfort zone, faced his fears and fulfilled his destiny.

I want you to write down twenty things that frighten you, or circumstances you have avoided, to make life easy, and each day commit to facing these fears. Exposure therapy is the best remedy. You will soon realise that your fears were illusions, as you step forward into your greatest life. Your biggest life lives on the other side of your fears. Listen to your heart. It's your life compass. Listen to it every day, and it will lead you in the direction of your dreams.

Commit to accomplishing five things every day in your pursuit of happiness. Commit to making it happen by taking maximum action each day. When you take 5 steps each day in the direction of your dreams, it equates to 35 per week – that's 140 every month, a total of 1680 each year. When you take 1680 steps in the direction of your dreams, every year, you will need a telescope to look back and see where you once were.

These steps are inward steps. Meditate, love, eat natural foods, exercise, be grateful, forgive, smile, contribute, dance and let the magic begin. See everything that happens in your life as a challenge, not a problem. Look for the goodness in all situations, and I promise you, that is all you will discover.

In the Vortex of Consciousness, my next book, I will give you a foolproof plan for binging into fruition what Archangel Gabriel refers to, as the rising of the new dawn. Times ahead are challenging, rewarding and exciting. Use your power. Journey towards the light and prepare yourself for the coming of the Vortex of Consciousness.

Spend as much time in nature as you can. Take your shoes off, connect with Mother Earth and share your energies. Hug at least three trees every week for several minutes and truly love them, feel their vibration. Spend time near water – the power that water gives you is immense. If you're a meat eater, try slowly coming off it, or take the plunge altogether if you wish. Start juicing every morning and giving your body what it needs to flourish. Be in the sunlight as often as possible. Sun gazing is a topic we will cover in detail, in the Vortex of Consciousness, along with a multitude of other ancient techniques that must be brought back into this modern world, if we, as a global community, are to bring peace back to our planet, back into our home.

Try and communicate with your angels and spirit guides. They are there, always, watching over you. Invite them closer, into your heart and listen. They will offer you honesty, integrity and a world of knowledge.

One thing I do regularly is stand in places with extra dark and dense energy and blast light all over the area. We live in a world that has energy points, just like chakras on your body and some are light and vibrant, some are less so. You will start to feel as you move around and your vibration increases, that when you come into a place where the energy is not so good, your heart and chest may feel tight and you may get anxious. If it happens please thank the Universe for showing you this information and release the feelings and ask for them to be or see them turned into light and positivity and used for good wherever needed. You will get better and better at this the more you do it.

As a human being now living with conscious awareness it's important that you create a dimension of space whereby the forces of light can accumulate. Use your mind to send love and light far and wide. Use your mind and your ray of light to create space around other human beings that are struggling. Once you create space with loving energy you will give the human being in question the opportunity to feel a different vibration and you will allow his or her conscious attention to be known. Often people are bombarded by the darker forces and their frequencies at work, and as you know, shining light in a dark room will be enough to light the path of love. You are so powerful. It's time to carry the torch.

Always remember, however, before you can help others you must be in the perfect state of mind yourself. Don't try and help others unless you are filled up and overflowing with an abundance of love and feel perfect, radiating positive and harmonious energy. You will know when you are in that state of mind. It takes constant effort to remain there, so your daily affirmations and meditations are of the utmost importance. Fine tune yourself, every day, just like a mechanic tunes up a race car, keeping it functioning correctly and enhancing its performance. The more effort you put in, the bigger the reward, as the engine of your mind works in harmony, for the greatest good of all.

We must help all light workers open clear channels of communication, so that they can hear the messages and heavens calling. It's the smog that covers the planet, the smog that Mother Earth is breathing daily, that stops the clarity shining through. When we return to the telepathic way of communicating, dishonesty and fear will be no more. We are all capable of telepathy right now, so practise it yourself, with likeminded individuals and also by speaking to spirit.

If we light workers can be unafraid and live in a fearless society, by controlling our thoughts and thinking that of only good and pure thoughts, fear will disintegrate and our channels will open wider. Fear hinders the communication from above as many doubt what they are hearing, sometimes thinking it's their imagination. We must help them understand the truth and that is they are being spoken to with knowledge and wisdom that is from another place, another realm, one that's inherently linked to ours, and cares about our sprint for freedom, where a faultless world awaits us.

The life you are living right now will turn to one of paradise. The life that others see you living will inspire them also, to step into the place you are residing. Paradise is the new reality that humanity will come to understand and eventually live in.

Paradise is the spirit world through and through. A place where every being of light feels nothing but pure and unadulterated love, for every other being of light surrounding them. I am excited about the great possibilities of returning to spirit once again. My wife and both our children were once all one, part of the same soul. We split up to go our separate ways and learn many different, individual lessons, and now we have reunited in human form, so together we can inspire and motivate the planet, to awareness, of all the great and wonderful possibilities.

When you spread the message and talk to fellow human beings, reassure them that when they move on it will be to a beautiful place. There is nothing to fear, only that to look forward to and be happy and proud of what lies in store, as they will at some stage, when they so choose, return to spirit.

I will be spending many years here as Jerry Sargeant. I will not pass until my work is done and right now and can see myself living to at least two hundred and fifty years of age. We can live for as long as want. We are ageless. There is no such thing as age. It's a figment of our imagination, instilled into us when we were born and had a date of birth. Souls live a timeless existence, so bring back your power in this way also and start to believe in this truth once again, that you too will pass on, only when you decide you are ready.

We really do live in Paradise and where we go next is also Paradise. When you start unlocking and revealing your deep-seated path, within the files of your subconscious mind, you will, I'm sure, travel back to the Paradise I am talking about and you will see it in all its glory. It's so beautiful, really it is. You do not want to travel back to this dense place after you have been there; it's a culture shock. Coming back is part of our mission, however, and our duty to fulfil our life contract must be concluded. I am fulfilling mine and now you are doing the same.

Let's spread the word together. We make a great team, an alliance that has a relentless will to achieve and succeed and knows no other way but to bring the light back to all parts of the Universe. Luke Skywalker brought peace back to the galaxy with the use of the light side of the force. Did you think that was fiction? A story created to satisfy your needs and entertain you?

The makers of these films were guided by us beings of light just as we are guiding Jerry Sargeant right now to pass on these words of wisdom to you, and the rest of the light workers, waiting for this message. This message has been waiting in the depths of light and perfect minds. We have been waiting for the right light worker to get ready and prepare themselves and be in the right place to allow us to channel this information.

To all of the human race, we salute you.

To all light workers, we salute you.

To all spirit guides, angels, fairies and incarnated beings of light, we salute you.

To the channeller of this message, Jerry Sargeant, we salute you.

Let the love flow freely and fill your mind, body and soul with a white light that will carry you on your journey. Let the white light become you. Let the light of love and the message of peace, joy and happiness embed itself in your aura, your energy field. We are committed to you and you must commit to yourself, to do all that is necessary, and continue to carry this torch, so others too will find what you have found.

Create your space and live in the present moment.

Love and light.

Archangel Gabriel

Lightning Source UK Ltd.
Milton Keynes UK
UKOW05f0648120417

298943UK00011B/123/P